Introduction to

BATTLEFIELD
WEAPONS
SYSTEMS

and
TECHNOLOGY

Also from Brassey's - the Oldest Name in Defence Publishing

BATTLEFIELD WEAPONS SYSTEMS & TECHNOLOGY (book series)

General Editor: Colonel R G Lee OBE, Military Director of Studies at the Royal Military College of Science, Shrivenham, UK

This new series of course manuals is written by senior lecturing staff at RMCS, Shrivenham, one of the world's foremost Institutions for Military Science and its application. It provides a clear and concise survey of the complex systems spectrum of modern ground warfare for officers-in-training and volunteer reserves throughout the English-speaking world.

Volume I Tytler, Jones, Wormell & Thompson
ARMOURED FIGHTING VEHICLES, LOGISTIC VEHICLES & BRIDGING

Volume II Ryan
GUNS, MORTARS & ROCKETS

Volume III Goad & Halsey
AMMUNITION (INCLUDING MINES & GRENADES)

Volume IV McNaught
NUCLEAR, BIOLOGICAL & CHEMICAL WARFARE

Volume V Marchant-Smith & Haslam
SMALL ARMS & CANNONS

Volume VI Willcox, Slade & Ramsdale
COMMAND, CONTROL & COMMUNICATION (C^3)

Volume VII Roper, Rodgers, Fowler, James & Garland-Collins
SURVEILLANCE & TARGET ACQUISITION

Volume VIII Murphy, Garland-Collins, Mowat & Garnell
GUIDED WEAPONS (INCLUDING LIGHT ANTI-ARMOUR WEAPONS)

Volume IX Ward & Turner
MILITARY DATA-PROCESSING & MICROCOMPUTERS

For full details of these and future titles in the series, please contact your local Brassey's/Pergamon office.

RELATED TITLES OF INTEREST FROM PERGAMON

Fordham	HIGH EXPLOSIVES & PROPELLANTS (2nd ed.)
Garnell	GUIDED WEAPON CONTROL SYSTEMS (2nd ed.)
Koopman	SEARCH & SCREENING
Morris	INTRODUCTION TO COMMUNICATION, COMMAND & CONTROL SYSTEMS
Yinon & Zitrin	THE ANALYSIS OF EXPLOSIVES

Introduction to

BATTLEFIELD WEAPONS SYSTEMS

and TECHNOLOGY

R G LEE OBE

Military Director of Studies
Royal Military College of Science
Shrivenham, UK

BRASSEY'S PUBLISHERS LIMITED

a member of the Pergamon Group

OXFORD · NEW YORK · TORONTO
SYDNEY · PARIS · FRANKFURT

U.K.	BRASSEY'S PUBLISHERS LIMITED, a member of the Pergamon Group, Headington Hill Hall, Oxford OX3 0BW, England
U.S.A.	Pergamon Press Inc., Maxwell House, Fairview Park, Elmsford, New York 10523, U.S.A.
CANADA	Pergamon Press Canada Ltd., Suite 104, 150 Consumers Road, Willowdale, Ontario M2J 1P9, Canada
AUSTRALIA	Pergamon Press (Aust.) Pty. Ltd., P.O. Box 544, Potts Point, N.S.W. 2011, Australia
FRANCE	Pergamon Press SARL, 24 rue des Ecoles, 75240 Paris, Cedex 05, France
FEDERAL REPUBLIC OF GERMANY	Pergamon Press GmbH, 6242 Kronberg-Taunus, Hammerweg 6, Federal Republic of Germany

First edition 1981

British Library Cataloguing in Publication Data

Lee, R. G.
Introduction to battlefield weapons systems
and technology.
1. Weapons systems.
I. Title.
623.4   U104

ISBN 0-08-027043-3 (Hardcover)
ISBN 0-08-027044-1 (Flexicover)

Library of Congress Catalog Card no: 81-82518

The views expressed in the book are those of the author and not necessarily those of the Ministry of Defence of the United Kingdom.

Printed in Great Britain by A. Wheaton & Co. Ltd., Exeter

Preface

The Series

This series of books is written for those who wish to improve their knowledge of military weapons and equipment. It is equally relevant to professional soldiers, those involved in developing or producing military weapons or indeed anyone interested in the art of modern warfare.

All the texts are written in a way which assumes no mathematical knowledge and no more technical depth than would be gleaned from school days. It is intended that the books should be of particular interest to army officers who are studying for promotion examinations, furthering their knowledge at specialist arms schools or attending command and staff schools.

The authors of the books are all members of the staff of the Royal Military College of Science, Shrivenham, which is comprised from a unique blend of academic and military experts. They are not only leaders in the technology of their subjects, but are aware of what the military practitioner needs to know. It is difficult to imagine any group of persons more fitted to write about the application of technology to the battlefield.

The Introduction

This book, the Introduction, attempts to introduce the problem a fighting soldier has in delineating to the designer what he requires his weapon systems to do. It also introduces sufficient technology to allow the reader to understand what are the implications of the requirements he may demand. As such it is intended for those who wish to widen their professional military knowledge. The other volumes in the series then allow those who wish to deepen their knowledge to do so in the fields which are of interest to them.

Shrivenham. May 1981   Geoffrey Lee

Acknowledgements

When I came to analyse the source of the information I have used in the preparation of this book, it became obvious that it is an amalgam of a career's experience as a soldier and the teaching I have received from many dedicated lecturers and instructors during regimental service and on courses.

More recently, I owe much to my academic and military colleagues at the Royal Military College of Science, Shrivenham. They have been both kind in their encouragement and generous in their co-operation and advice on the content of my script.

Finally, my gratitude for many, many hours of loyal hard work on the full preparation of this script for printing, goes to my wife, Joy.

Contents

List of Illustrations

Chapter 3

Chapter 4

Chapter 7

1
Armoured Fighting Vehicles, Logistic Vehicles and Bridging

During the history of warfare, an equipment has often been produced to suit the tactics of the day and conversely sometimes tactics have changed to make maximum use of a new equipment. The tank can claim to have been involved in both developments. It was produced in 1917 to provide the answer to the tactical problem of breaking through trench systems heavily defended by machine gun fire and barbed wire. In 1940, by way of the thinking of General Fuller and Sir Basil Liddel Hart, through the trials and organisation of General Guderian, the Blitzkrieg tactics were largely designed to suit the characteristics of the tank.

The 1939 - 45 war may be looked upon, from one viewpoint, as a series of lessons in which tank formations outran their infantry or their logistic support. The Dunkirk evacuation was in part possible because the German tanks did not have the support of their infantry to cross the ditches and canals, which are a feature of the low lying ground around Dunkirk. The German tank formations, too, ground to a halt outside Moscow and short of Alexandria gasping for fuel and supplies.

In the East the Russians, like the Germans in 1940, again and again did not have the mechanised, or even motorised, infantry to keep up with the tank units. It became a major German tactic to separate the Russian infantry from their armour by the judicious use of artillery and small arms fire and then destroy the unsupported Russian tanks by anti-tank gun fire or by the use of tank guns.

During their defensive actions in Russia from 1942 - 45 the German Army learned that their tanks required high sustained tactical mobility to reach positions from which they could counter attack Russian armoured breakthroughs: in the spaces of Russia they could afford to give ground to gain time to group to do this. They also learned that their infantry must be at least motorised and, if possible, in armoured vehicles which could keep up with the tanks. Other nations followed suit and in the last year of the war infantry in German, Russian and Western Allied armies were all using armoured vehicles; sometimes these were tanks with their turrets removed, to carry their infantry. The logistic lesson had also, to some extent, been solved, often by the use of massive transport support as in the case of the

1

American Army.

Meanwhile the British in the West were slow to realise that the Germans were
adept at destroying the British tanks with their anti-tank weapons while keeping
their own tank formations intact for that role at which they excel - shock action.
Both the British and United States pre-occupation became a determination not to
be up-armoured or out-gunned, which had been their lot throughout the war.

Since that time the lessons have been re-learned in the Middle East wars. The
Syrians paid the penalty for having too few infantry in the Golan Heights, and an
Israeli Brigade was brought up short in the Sinai when it was caught unsupported
by infantry in a trap of Egyptian anti-tank guided weapons (ATGW). It also became
evident more than ever before what an immense expenditure of ammunition and
equipment modern warfare caused: the logistic back-up had to be larger than ever
previously envisaged.

Fig. 1 Chieftain 55 tonnes tank with a 120 mm gun

Different armies have drawn different lessons from their wars. The British, and
to a lesser extent the Americans, wished to avoid being out-gunned and up-
armoured as had happened against the Germans throughout the 1939 - 45 war. As
a result the relatively heavily armoured, big gunned Centurions and Chieftains,
M48s and M60s have been the post-war trend in these countries. The Chieftain,
which is the current extreme of this type of tank in service, is a 55 tonnes tank

with a 120 mm gun.

The Israelis favour heavily protected tanks in the desert, which has little foliage cover but good visibility and frequent long ranges; they have developed their own Merkava tank which weighs approximately 56 tonnes, has a very narrow turret and its engine at the front which gives extra protection.

Fig. 2 56 tonnes Israeli Merkava tank with 105 mm gun

The Germans learned that they needed sustained tactical mobility to re-group quickly to oppose armoured thrusts: so they accepted that protection could be partly achieved by fast motoring from cover to cover. The result was the Leopard 1 of 40 tonnes (see Fig. 3). The Russians, too, believe in the ability to motor long distances on roads at good speeds and have reasonable mobility across country. This is a consequence of their policy of fast advances along narrow axes.

If different nations develop different types of tank for the same sort of warfare over the same terrain, there must be some reason why there is not an optimum attractive design answer. It may be worth looking at the requirement as seen by the user - the fighting soldier.

THE FIGHTING SOLDIERS REQUIREMENT

The mainstream of tank tactics during the 1939 - 45 war and since has led all nations towards a Main Battle Tank (MBT) which can fight a breakthrough battle with the infantry and then exploit that breakthrough, with infantry support, by developing swift advances into enemy held territory. It is important to maintain the momentum of the attack to prevent the defender regrouping and regaining his control and balance.

Fig. 3 40 tonnes West German Leopard 1 tank

During the breakthrough phase of the battle, the tank will require good protection to withstand anti-tank attack, a good set of armaments to fight through defensive positions and good battlefield mobility in which vehicle agility is inherent. During the exploitation phase good sustained tactical mobility is the essential feature.

However, in defence, an armoured force cannot remain unused. If there are insufficient effective anti-tank weapons, the requirement is for tanks to defeat the attacker's tanks. Such a role demands good protection, effective armament and agility; these characteristics are the same as those required for the break-through battle. Other requirements, however, are necessary. A defender will never have sufficient armour, spread along the Forward Edge of the Battle Area (FEBA), to deal with the attacker who has concentrated his forces in one place for a break-through. In this case good tactical mobility is once again necessary on roads and tracks to motor the tank to oppose the attempted breakthrough, or even to contain the enemy's exploitation of that breakthrough. This was the lesson the Germans learned so thoroughly in Russia.

From these requirements it becomes obvious that there are three main character-istics which must be balanced in a well designed tank:

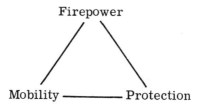

Fig. 4 Interplay of design characteristics

At first the greatest difference between an intending attacker's tank and that of an intending defender would appear to be that an attacker requires good mobility for exploitation at the expense of protection, but this argument falls down when the requirement for the breakthrough battle is considered, during which there may be a slogging match. It falls down again when the defender's requirement for tactical mobility is acknowledged; indeed the defender needs to move more quickly than the attacker. The balance becomes even more complicated when it is realised that a highly mobile and agile tank moving fast from bound to bound on the battle-field gains some protection by making the attacking anti-tank weapon gunner's or ATGW operator's job more difficult. It is this last argument, added to the tact-ical mobility requirement, which formed much of the rationale behind the design of the lightly armoured Leopard 1 tank; but it was not the view of the British or Americans and indeed it is not the view of the Israelis. Obviously the fighting soldier's requirement is complex and the designer can not provide the ideal tank for him. The soldier must compromise, but to achieve the best compromise he should first understand the designer's problem.

DESIGNING A TANK

Protection and Weight Limits

The limits on the size and weight of tanks are set by the necessity for tanks to be moved by rail and road. The height of bridges and tun-nels, the width of available wagon flats and the normal necessity for two trains to pass each other are the rail limitations. The rail temp-late or guage, within which the outline of the tank must fit is the manifestation of those limitations. An example is the TZ gauge used for military vehicle movement on the contin-ent. See Fig. 5.

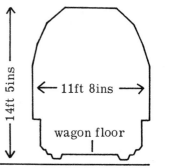

Fig. 5 TZ Continental gauge

If tanks are to be transported at all by rail, and it is difficult to see how they could all arrive in the battle zone without being so, they must be put on rail flats either in normal times or in a period of tension which may lead to conflict. So this need sets the outer size limits.

On the other hand the main limitation imposed by road movement is that of weight

and the weight limiting factor is the strength of the bridges to be crossed. The
more bridges a tank can cross the more mobile it is within the theatre of operations. If a tank can cross bridges with a classification of 50 tonnes, then it is
able to use more roads than if its weight limits it to using roads with bridges with
classifications of 60 tonnes. It should be remembered, too, that the heavier the
tank the stronger, and heavier, must be the bridging equipment which the engineer support provides. The whole problem is compounded if the tank must be
moved by transporter: the total road weight of the tank on a transporter goes up
to 80 tonnes or more.

Height Restraints

Within rail and road movement constraints it is tactically important to reduce the
height of a tank as much as possible to provide as low a silhouette and as small a
target as possible. It is also desirable to keep the weight as low as possible to
ensure that the pressure on the vehicle's track is kept to a minimum: this has a
significant effect on the vehicle's ability to cross soft ground.

The designer faces several restrictions which determine height:

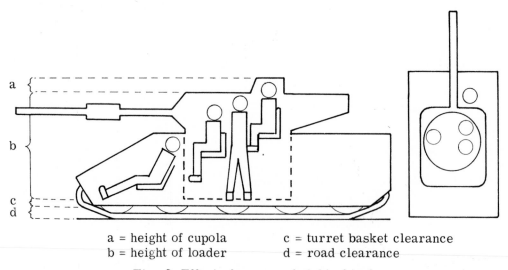

        a = height of cupola   c = turret basket clearance
        b = height of loader   d = road clearance

           Fig. 6 Effect of crew on height of tank

The first is the height from the sole of the boot to the top of the helmet of the
loader when standing (b). In a tank he must stand to load the heavy ammunition.
To his height must be added, at the top, the height above the turret required by
the optics of the Commander's cupola (a). At the bottom, more height is allowed
for ground clearance (d): this measurement is determined by the user, based on
the risk he is prepared to take on bellying in soft ground. Russian tanks do not
have a turret basket with a floor, but for mine protection reasons, Western tanks
do: this again adds a small amount to the height (c).

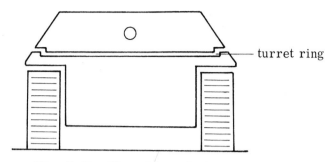

Fig. 7 Position of turret ring

The second factor which may affect the overall height is the height of the turret
ring added to the height of the gun breech when the gun is at maximum depression.
The turret ring height depends on the width of the tank. The width is normally a
function of tactical mobility such as its ability to move through trees and down
narrow streets: most tanks are approximately 3. 20 m to 3. 70 m wide. The difficulty with such a width is that turret rings of modern tanks are of too great a diameter to sit within the tracks, so they must be set above them as shown in Fig. 7.

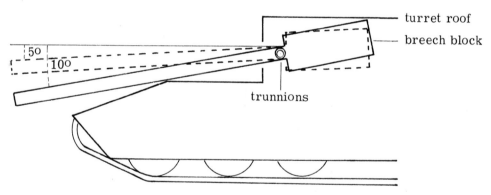

Fig. 8 Effect of gun depression on height

The gun pivots vertically on the trunnions: by referring to Fig. 8 it can be seen
that the further the gun is depressed the higher is the top of the breech and it is
this which decides the height of the turret roof. Russian tanks have a depression
of approximately 90 mil (5^0) but most Western tanks increase this to approximately 180 mil (10^0). Fig. 9, at the top of the next page, shows that depression has a
considerable effect on the amount of the full frontal a tank exposes when engaging
a target from a hull down position.

Weight Restraints

Height is not only important for tactical reasons, but for weight and protection
reasons as well. The smaller the tank, the less volume needs to be protected

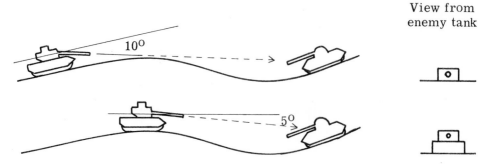

Fig. 9 Effect of gun depression on tank exposure

with armour and the lighter the tank will be. A general idea of what makes up the
internal volume of a four man turreted tank is:

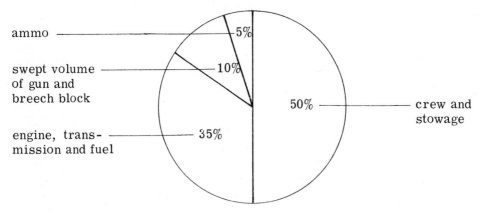

Fig. 10 Analysis of volume

It is the volume and weight, together with the degree of mobility required, which
control the overall size and weight of the tank.   The weight of a four man turreted
tank is roughly divided up as:

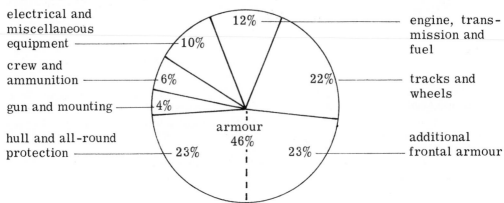

Fig. 11 Analysis of weight

Twenty-three per cent of the weight is in the thickened frontal armour. If the front silhouette of the tank could be reduced, then the weight of the armour could be reduced by a considerable amount. There are two interesting tank designs in which this has been done. The Russians in their T72 and T64 have removed the loader altogether and replaced him with a mechanical autoloader: the height imposed by the standing loader thus disappears. Instead it is now decided by the height of the turret ring added to the turret height which is imposed by the gun depression. The result is a reduction in height and volume. As the depression of the gun is only approximately 90 mil (5°) the compromise is now well on the side of a lower silhouette. Further volume saving is also made by having small crewmen, said to be a maximum of 5' 4" tall, so the overall weight of armour is reduced. Because there is less weight a smaller engine is possible, giving a smaller engine compartment to be armoured. Also the reduction in weight allows smaller and lighter tracks. The final result is a tank which weighs some 41 tonnes only.

Fig. 12 The 41 tonnes Russian T72 tank

The second tank design to result in a much reduced weight, without sacrificing protection, approached the problem in a different way: it is that of the Swedish S tank which has no turret at all. The gun is fixed in the front of the hull and laid, both laterally and vertically, by using a finely controlled suspension system. By this method it can be depressed to the desirable 180 mil (10°). It has an automatic loader and a three man crew: the commander always fires the gun, and the third crew member is used only for driving in reverse: the tank motors as well in reverse as forward. Because it is very low indeed and has no turret, the S tank has a high level of frontal protection and only weighs approximately 38 tonnes. With the aid of a flotation screen it can even swim.

Fig. 13 The 38 tonnes Swedish S tank

We have already seen that the volume of the engine is important and that it is obviously closely related to its power. Indeed the designer's closed loop from which it is hard to escape is:

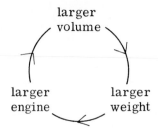

larger
volume

larger
engine

larger
weight

Fig. 14 The designer's closed loop

So far we have only mentioned armour in general. In practice, design of armour is very much determined by the threat. Rolled Homogeneous Armour (RHA) steel has been the conventional armour. Until the Russian T34 appeared on the battlefield in 1941 and proved itself the most advanced tank of its day, not much attention had been paid to sloping armour. However, the Germans were quick to copy

the Russians and sloped armour has been a feature of tanks ever since.   The S
tank and the T72 make maximum use of it today.   The advantages can be seen
easily in Fig. 15.

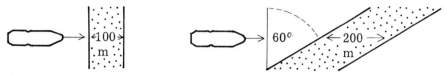
Fig. 15 Sloped armour effect

Not only does sloping the armour at 60° double the distance a projectile must
penetrate, assuming it arrives horizontally, but it has a chance of causing it to
ricochet.   The designer's aim is to ensure that the hull and turret are sloped to
the greatest possible extent.   The T72 and S tank have achieved a high degree of
slope on their hulls and the Chieftain has done the same on its turret.   Sloped
armour is still the main method of defending against kinetic energy (KE) attack,
though the use of ceramics in the future could improve the performance.

One of the designer's main problems is to provide protection against the highly
penetrative HEAT warheads, particularly as they are used on most ATGW.   In
recent years compound armours, developed first at the British Military Vehicle
Experimental Establishment (MVEE) at Chobham, have been adopted by Western
nations and are being fitted on their new tanks.   Their effect is to degrade the
performance of HEAT attack considerably.   They will also degrade the effect of
HESH.   How they achieve it is classified.

It has always been possible to defeat HESH by spaced or sandwich armour.   A
glance at Chapter 3 will show that the action of HESH requires a solid piece of
steel armour to carry the shock wave which produces the scabbing effect.   Spaced
or sandwich armour would result in a scabbing of the outside layer only.   On the
other hand, the effect of the explosion on the outside of the tank may cause sufficient damage to external elements of the tank, and to the crew, to put it and
them out of the battle.

We have looked at ways of reducing the volume and weight.   Now let us consider
mobility which is closely related to the engine size.

Mobility

We have noted that strategic mobility is mainly related to restrictions on the tank
size to allow it to be carried by rail or on roads.   Tactical mobility is its ability
to move under its own steam over some distance, within the theatre of operations.
Battlefield mobility is reasonably self explanatory, but it includes the agility required to get in and out of fire positions and to move from bound to bound and
cover to cover; clearly the time a tank is exposed to enemy fire is closely related
to its battlefield mobility.

The main factors which determine mobility are firstly the power output of the
engine in relation to the weight of the tank, known as power to weight ratio;

secondly the ability of the suspension to withstand the rattling it will sustain across
country and even more its ability to smooth out the ride to make it possible for
the crew to withstand the cross country travel; thirdly the design of the tracks
which determines the grip on the ground and the ground pressure exerted through
the tracks and finally the ability of the tank to cross gaps, climb slopes and step-
ups.

The power to weight ratio of the Chieftain Mk V is 11.6 kilowatt per kilonewton
(kW/kN) which can be translated into 15.5 brake horse power per ton (BHP/t)·
the American M60 A1 is 11.8 kW/kN (15.8 BHP/t). These power to weight ratios
reflect the United States and British bias towards protection rather than mobility.
The Leopard I in which the bias is reversed is 15.4 kW/kN (21 BHP/t). These
ratios were obtained from diesel engines giving a maximum horsepower in the
region of 750 to 850. Now there has been a quantum jump in the power output of
tank engines. In the British Challenger and German Leopard II case the power is
obtained from turbo-charged diesel engines giving about 1,200 hp and 1,500 hp.
In the American XM1 case a similar power is obtained from a gas turbine engine.
The result is power to weight ratios in the region of 19 - 22 kW/kN (25 - 30 BHP/t).
Such power allows greater battlefield agility and greater tactical mobility. This
will permit shorter exposure times, faster re-grouping and faster advance after
a breakthrough. A gas turbine engine can produce more power for a given size
than a diesel, but it has a much higher fuel consumption resulting in larger fuel
tanks. It is expected, however, that it will be possible, in future gas turbines, to
reduce the heavy consumption.

To achieve the best tactical mobility, a designer would design his tracks so that
they could withstand long road travel without tearing up the road for following
transport, and his gearing ratios so that they could achieve high sustained road
speeds. To obtain the best battlefield agility his tracks would need to be a different shape to grip earth and the gear ratios higher to give the acceleration and hill
climbing performance which is so necessary. There are indications in the designs
that while Western countries have a bias towards battlefield performance, Russia
emphasises tactical mobility.

Suspensions have improved in parallel with engines. The American XM1 and
German Leopard II, by the use of conventional suspensions, have been able to
make use of the higher speeds produced by their more powerful engines. The
most advanced and complicated suspension yet designed into an in service tank is
the hydropneumatic system in the 'S' tank. Its very fine control is necessary to
lay the gun. It is still important, however, to keep an eye on the ability of the
crew to withstand fast cross country motoring: this is still the limiting factor for
sustained cross country travel.

When travelling cross country, the design of the tracks is important. In general
in Europe, an 'aggressive tread' is required to grip the ground, which conflicts
with the tactical mobility requirement for smoother tracks with rubber pads.
The Leopard tanks accept the double requirement by incorporating a facility for
the crew to change some of the rubber pads for steel grousers to give a better
grip.

Whichever type of track is used a most important characteristic to affect the cross
country performance is the ground pressure exerted by the vehicle through the

track. This determines how much it will sink in soft ground. As a rough guide, vehicles with a ground pressure of over 105 kN/m^2 (15 lb per sq in) are confined to roads and good tracks; vehicles with a pressure of 40 kN/m^2 (6 lb per sq in) can cross peat. Chieftain's ground pressure is 93.2 kN/m^2 (13.5 lb per sq in) which means that it cannot cross all European agricultural land, but the M60 at 76.5 kN/m^2 (11.1 lb per sq in) could cross most, as could the Leopard I which has a slightly higher ground pressure of 84 kN/m^2 (12.2 lb per sq in). The Scorpion tracked Recce Vehicle has an excellent cross country ability with its pressure of 34.5 kN/m^2 (5 lb per sq in).

While ground pressures are unlikely to change much to give better cross country performance, the engine power and the suspension have already improved greatly over the past two decades, giving an increase both in the tactical and battlefield mobility of modern tanks coming into service such as the XM1, Leopard II and Challenger. At the same time quite important steps have been taking place in the firepower field.

Firepower

In this chapter, we will look only briefly at the firepower developments in tank design. The outline gun design is dealt with in Chapter 2 and the all important question of ammunition in Chapter 3.

The German 88 mm was probably the most famous anti-tank gun in the 1939 - 45 war and since then the most successful tank gun has been the British 105 mm. It has been fitted to most Western tanks, including the Centurion, the M60, the Leopard I and XM1. The Israelis liked it so much that they fitted it to their captured T54s and T62s. It can fire APDS rounds, HE, HESH, Smoke and Beehive anti-personnel rounds. Since the introduction of the Chieftain tank, Britain has fielded a 120 mm gun which has separated ammunition. It is rifled and can fire APDS, APFSDS, HESH, HEAT and Smoke rounds.

After their rifled 100 mm gun on their T55 tank the Russians have favoured smooth bore guns with the 115 mm on the T62 and a 125 mm on the T72. The advantages of the smooth bore gun, apart from its simplicity of manufacture, is its comparative lightness and its ability to fire, at very high muzzle velocities, the fin stabilised APFSDS rounds. Fin stabilisation, and so the smooth bore gun, also suits the HEAT hollow charge round which is rendered less effective if spun (see Chapter 3). The West Germans also recognised the advantages of a smooth bore and have adopted a 120 mm version for their Leopard II tank. In their turn the United States intend to fit it in their later XM1 models, to replace the 105 mm gun. The British intend to maintain a 120 mm rifled gun in Chieftain and the new Challenger in the belief that it is more flexible, being able to fire spin stabilised HESH as well as APFSDS and HEAT. There is an advantage to be gained because the Warsaw Pact countries must then continue to protect against a wider spectrum of armour attack. On the other hand the advantages of standardisation within NATO are lost.

As important to the guns effect as the design of the gun itself has been the development of Improved Fire Control Systems (IFCS). Range estimation was the first element of it to be incorporated, and although it is not very important for

KE attack with its flat trajectory, it is very important for HEAT and especially
for HESH projectiles with their lower muzzle velocities and higher trajectories.
The Laser Range Finder (LRF) has removed the problem of range estimation.
The addition of a computer can result in automatic adjustments on the sight graticule to allow for such errors as gun jump, bore wear, different types of ammunition, wind direction and velocity, temperature of the air and the ammunition
propellant. It can even allow for the crossing speed of a target. It is an enormous
step forward in the effectiveness of a tank's firepower. Most modern Western
tanks will have an IFCS incorporating all or some of these capabilities.

Future Developments

Fig. 16 External gun concept

The British Army have conducted a trial with the 'S' tank and have found it did not
meet the tactical requirement of a Main Battle Tank. Nevertheless, the need for
a radical review of tank design is near. The XM1, Challenger and Leopard II
have all taken their respective nation to a heavier tank than they had previously
and all have made full use of increased engine power and improved suspension.
Indeed the three nations are much nearer in their tank concepts than they have
been for the past twenty years. They may well all be 55 tonnes or more, with
improved protection, improved mobility and, when the XM1 is up-gunned to
120 mm gun, improved firepower. But the warning bell must be sounded about

weight.   The three tanks are reaching a limit beyond which their tactical mobility
will be impaired as the number of routes they will be able to use is reduced.   In
addition their battlefield mobility will be degraded as their ground pressure increases.   The most fruitful path to follow to lose weight is to cut down the frontal
armour by reducing the height.   One way is to follow the S tank path.   Another is
to cut the crew to three, put in an autoloader and follow the T72 path.   Yet another,
which may be possible in the future with the improvement in fibre optical systems,
would be to adopt an external gun concept.   In this case there would be no turret,
just a revolving gun on top of the hull as portrayed in the AAI corporation's sug-
gestion for a rapid deployment force which is shown in Fig. 16.

Such an approach would reduce the crew to two or three men.   It would necessarily
suffer from reduced vision; it would also involve the use of an automatic loader,
which probably cuts down the natures of ammunition which could be used to two;
it would also be difficult to deal with misfires.   On the other hand, apart from a
dramatic reduction in weight, it would present a very small target when hull
down.

Before leaving the tank designer's problems, mention should be made that many
soldiers do not believe that the crew can be reduced from four men.   They consider that a smaller number could not maintain a tank in battle.   If a reduction
were considered, the designer would be asked to ensure that the new tank would
be easier to maintain and replenish as well as being more reliable than those of
the current generation.

Of course, some say that the day of the tank is numbered.   With their improvement in performance, armour and armament, it is sometimes asserted that
helicopters could replace tanks.

Fig. 17 Russian Hind Gun Ship

HELICOPTERS AND THEIR CAPABILITIES

It is not intended to discuss the general capabilities of helicopters, but only to consider how they impinge on mechanised warfare. The United States demonstrated in Vietnam that helicopters could be used to lay down neutralising fire with rockets and machine guns; the Russians have used their Hind "gun ships" (Fig. 17) in Afghanistan; but as yet no nation has experience of using helicopters as weapon platforms in all out general war.

From reading, it would appear that Russia intends to use its gun ships aggressively to seek out and destroy targets. So far it would appear they would have only the capability to take on lightly armoured or soft targets with machine gun fire, 57 mm rocket fire and bombs. No doubt such fire could be reasonably effective if it could be brought to bear accurately but it is difficult to see that the neutralising rockets or bombs, due to the limited ammunition helicopters can carry, would be so effective as artillery fire to support frontal attacks. Their great value would be in the support of troops operating beyond the range of their artillery, which is the role given to Russia's airborne and heliborne troops. The American Advanced Attack Helicopter (AAH), now under development, is to be fitted with 20 mm cannon; such a weapon may improve both its attack capability and its ability to defend itself. It is also so designed to be less vulnerable than current helicopters to attack from guns with calibres up to approximately 20 mm. However, helicopters

Fig. 18 German Gepard air defence vehicle

are vulnerable to fire from costly anti-aircraft vehicles such as the Russian ZSU 23/4 and German Gepard (Fig. 18), because the distinctive rotor blade signatures can be picked up on the target acquisition radars. They are also vulnerable to some man-portable air defence weapons, though they can be protected against heat seeking missiles. They are not so easily hit as may be imagined to other types of fire unless they are caught in the hover position, landing or taking off. As yet, it does not appear that the helicopter gun ship could replace the tank's ability to fight a breakthrough battle, but perhaps they could be useful if not devastating in the exploitation stage.

On the other hand United States experience in Vietnam, followed by trials and studies in the United Kingdom, the United States and West Germany, have indicated that helicopters firing ATGW, such as the European Hot, the American Tow or the Russian Spiral, may be very effective indeed against advancing tanks. Each helicopter may be able to take out several tanks before being destroyed itself.

Fig. 19 United States helicopter AH-1S Cobra armed with Tow ATGW

Both the Warsaw Pact and NATO countries envisage helicopters being used extensively in the anti-tank role, so as a counter, we may now see the development of an anti-helicopter vehicle, ground based or airborne, to counter them. This could lead towards an escort vehicle for tanks and Armoured Personnel Carriers (APCs) to deal with enemy APCs and Mechanised Infantry Carrier Vehicles

(MICVs) as well as helicopters. Such vehicles, however, would most probably be
as expensive as the ZSU 23/4 or Gepard, because they would need radar or
thermal imaging to locate low flying or hovering helicopters. There is no doubt
that helicopters will be deeply involved in the mechanised warfare of the future.
The immediate British contribution is the Lynx armed with Tow, while the
United States have their Bell AH-1S Cobras also equipped with Tow.

In addition to their gunship and anti-tank roles, most nations envisage the use of
helicopters to insert troops in the enemy's rear areas to cause disruption, move
them quickly to counter enemy attacks or exploit situations. When helicopters
are used as troop carriers in such roles, they replace and fulfil part of the
function of APCs or MICVs.

APCs AND MICVs

Fig. 20 West German Marder MICV

All nations with mechanised forces accept the need for an armoured vehicle to
carry infantry and keep up with advancing tank forces. After the 1939 - 45 war
most Warsaw Pact and NATO nations developed APCs with top protection. On the
whole, like the British FV 432 and the Russian BTR 50, they carried a section of
infantry and were tracked. They normally were amphibious. Their role was to

carry infantry, to protect them from shell splinters and to a lesser extent from small arms fire. The British FV 432 also incorporated a NBC protection system, which was a new facility for infantry soldiers.

In 1967 the Russians introduced their BMP, which was the first proper MICV to be fielded. It has a cupola and mounts both a 76 mm low pressure gun and a Sagger ATGW. This was followed in 1971 by the West German production of the Marder, which mounts a 20 mm cannon in its turret: more recently the Milan ATGW has been fitted, although it cannot be fired from under armour.

The development of MICVs has brought into question how mechanised infantry will fight. It is often loosely stated that Russian and German mechanised infantry are taught to fight from their vehicles whilst the British are not. Indeed the individual weapon gun ports in the side of the BMP and Marder are used as evidence to support this view. Such generalisations are dangerous and it is worthwhile looking at what the mechanised infantry want from their APCs or MICVs.

The first requirement is to carry the infantry and their equipment in vehicles which will keep up with tanks. It obviously makes sense to provide protection from artillery splinters and today that means from 152 mm and 155 mm shells. Such protection not only provides for survival from enemy artillery but allows infantry in the attack to follow up their own artillery very closely. This require-ment is often referred to as the "Battle Taxi" role. However, there is a con-flict in the requirement, even for such a simple vehicle concept. The two sides of the argument are enshrined in the BMP and Marder. These vehicles are of a comparable length and width, and even though the Marder is much higher, this does not account for the difference in weight between the BMP at approximately 16 tonnes and Marder at approximately 29 tonnes. The reason is that the BMP is only lightly protected, certainly it is not proof against near 155 mm shell bursts: but it is amphibious. The Marder is extremely well protected, but the resultant weight prevents it from swimming. The value of being able to swim in the Central European area is again the cause of much heated discussion. Most rivers in this part of the world have soft or steep banks which make entry, and particularly exit, difficult. It is this feature which throws into doubt what would otherwise appear to be a useful capability for an APC or MICV.

Next, the requirement to carry equipment should not be undervalued. If an infan-try section can carry a few days food, rapid cratering charges, radios, small arms, anti-armour weapons and a good supply of ammunition for them, it then possesses much greater flexibility than a section with only immediate battle necessities. It is perhaps important to note that within a given sized vehicle, more equipment stowage space is available if room is not provided for the infantry to move themselves and their weapons about to fire from weapon ports. Firing from ports means a larger vehicle and is not very effective, but, on the other hand, it may be good for morale and keep the infantryman in touch with the battle.

The next big question which produces the big complication in the requirements is the armament to be put on an armoured infantry carrier. One strongly held point of view is that there should be no armament provided on an APC and it should remain a battle taxi. There is no doubt that there is a possibility that an APC, when it becomes a MICV, may become involved in fire fights with enemy AFVs and so endanger the survival of the infantry section it carries. There is also a conflict over the use of the vehicle when the infantry section is dismounted in a defensive position: if the vehicle were sited in a position where it could use its firepower it would not normally be placed well for the swift embussing and movement of the section: there would also be a possibility that the vehicle would be destroyed and the section stranded.

The Russians, the West Germans and Americans have all opted for the advantages which the added firepower will provide for their fighting units. The United States Infantry Fighting Vehicle (IFV) will mount a 25 mm cannon and the Tow ATGW which will be fired from under armour. Obviously these nations view the infantry's capability to defeat the enemy's armour as a high priority. The British MICV, which will be one of the Mechanised Combat Vehicle (MCV 80) family, will most probably mount a 25 mm or 30 mm cannon but not an ATGW. It will thus have an anti-APC/MICV capability but not an anti-tank capability.

The anti-air capability of APC/MICVs is not strongly stressed except in the case of the Marder which can angle its gun upwards to 1,080 mil (60°). It is unlikely that machine guns or cannons will have much chance of shooting down a modern fighter ground attack (FGA) aircraft, but a regiment of Marder may deter air attack, including helicopter ATGW attack. However, for effective aircraft engagement, advanced radar or thermal imaging acquisition and tracking systems are necessary.

It is very much the province of the soldier to decide what capabilities he requires of his APCs or MICVs. The more options which can be provided on the vehicles the more flexible they will be. There is a danger that those responsible for stating the requirements will imagine that they can dictate exactly how they can be used: this can only be the province of the unit commander in the field. Ideally the vehicle should be designed to give that commander the maximum number of possible options. There are, however, design, manpower and, inevitably, cost restraints. The soldier must be clear in his own mind as to what trade-offs he is prepared to accept before he can give the designer a clear directive for his minimum requirements.

RECONNAISSANCE VEHICLES

Reconnaissance in a defensive role covers a wide band of activities. It could entail mere observation and reporting, which involves no sought for aggressive contact. It could involve the defining of the axes of the main enemy thrusts which would require the need to neutralise or obstruct the enemy's reconnaissance forces. Finally it could entail the delaying of an enemy's advance which would involve serious fighting. In Europe, where there is little ground to give up, it is possible that the Western nations reconnaissance forces could be quickly involved in fighting to cause delay.

In the advance the same spectrum would be covered and it is very possible that reconnaissance troops would need to fight to get worthwhile information about the enemy's dispositions.

Before deciding on a reconnaissance vehicle's ability to fight, the main requirement is a good surveillance system: a mixture of radar, thermal imaging, image intensification and powerful optical devices is ideal, but cost normally rules out the ideal: a compromise must be accepted.   Then a good radio to ensure that the information gained by fast secure means is the next essential.   These two factors form the basic needs of any reconnaissance vehicle.   From then on the balance of mobility, protection and firepower depends on the role of the reconnaissance troops and the terrain over which they will fight.

A very basic mobility decision is whether the vehicle should be tracked or wheeled and there has been much heated discussion on this subject.   There does not appear to be a general concensus.   At present in Europe, West Germany fields the Spahpanzer Luchs which is an 8 x 8 wheeled vehicle while the British use the tracked Scorpion and Scimitar.   The USSR tend to use a mixture of MBTs and BMPs, so they are track-borne.

If it is envisaged that a recce vehicle will operate on roads more than cross country in Central Europe, then a wheeled vehicle holds the advantage.   The converse is also true: tracked vehicles would hold the advantage if heavy going cross country performance were the main criterion.   In desert country wheels are often better than tracks - but even then there are forms of desert where the converse is true.   The only basis on which the soldier can make his decision on whether he wants wheels or tracks is thorough analysis of the ground over which he expects his reconnaissance troops to operate.

Fig. 21 West German Spahpanzer Luchs

If a heavy vehicle is required, with good protection and good firepower, it will almost certainly be a tracked vehicle. With the constraints imposed by size and mobility, it is virtually impossible to design a wheeled vehicle of more than 25 tonnes. The ground pressure, even though spread over eight wheels, as it is in the Spahpanzer Luchs, would be too great to allow it any reasonable cross country performance.

If this analysis is accepted it appears that NATO in Central Europe, operating in an area of damp heavy agricultural land, with little chance of trading ground to gain tactical advantage, should tend towards a need for tracked vehicles able to fight a delaying battle. In other areas, such as deserts or in terrains where vehicles are confined to roads, and the trading of ground may be possible, lighter wheeled vehicles will have the advantage. Of course the ideal terrain for one particular type of vehicle never exists: so the discussion continues.

LOGISTIC VEHICLE FLEET

Since the German army in the early 1940s first learned the importance of a good logistic vehicle fleet to back up mechanised forces, the logistic requirement has increased both in bulk and importance.

It has never been possible for a nation to design a tailor made logistic fleet to carry its combat loads from base areas to fighting troops. During and after the 1939 - 45 war many individual vehicles were designed specifically for military uses and then, bought surplus, adapted to civilian use. Now the emphasis is re-versed, there is such a huge civilian market, worldwide, for rugged load carry-ing vehicles, which are able to cover rough ground, that they can be used directly for military purposes or be adapted to do so.

The three main characteristics of logistic vehicles, which dictate their suitability are adequate mobility, sufficient load carrying capacity and ease of loading and unloading.

Mobility

It is now generally agreed that, except for the very forward areas, it is too costly to develop special military logistic vehicles. A large European nation may need over 100,000 logistic vehicles for its army: so there are obvious huge economic, repair and spares savings to be made if civilian vehicles can be adapted.

Most nations, including West Germany and the United Kingdom, classify their logistic vehicles into various grades of mobility and then buy suitable civilian vehicles to fulfil them. As an example the United Kingdom uses three grades, which start in the rear areas with Low Mobility Load Carriers (LMLC): these vehicles are not expected to move far off roads, except to take cover from air and are required to carry heavy palletised loads. Medium Mobility Load Carriers (MMLC) are required to operate in operational areas to carry out the duties of second and third line transport: their duties require them to negotiate such hazards as muddy tracks in woods and river banks adjacent to bridges and ferry sites and some of them may be required to run their palletised loads to fighting units such as gun battery positions. It is in the field of High Mobility Load Carriers (HMLC) that the requirement is the most difficult to define. Britain currently has the Stalwart HMLC 6 x 6, 5 tonnes to fulfil the need; it can carry stores, ammunition and fuel pods across most country which can be traversed by AFVs; it can also swim.

Fig. 22 Stalwart HMLC with CALM

The United States have their M 548 tracked carrier with a 5 tonnes load carrying capability based on the M 113 APC and a tracked stores carrier, based on the M 109 SP gun chassis, has been developed (see Fig. 23 on the next page).

These types of vehicles are near to achieving the best possible mobility, but they are expensive. They are also not such good load carriers as trucks. On the other hand West Germany has based its requirement mainly on the premise that it will fight in its own country, where it has a well built network of roads almost every-where. It believes it has a need for only a few HMLCs.

Load carrying Ability

The last two decades have seen a revolution in the civilian cargo load carrying world. It is mainly based on the development of palletised loads, containers and

Mechanical Handling Equipment (MHE). Within a theatre of operations, palletisation has strongly affected military logistics. It permits swift handling and reduces the manpower required to handle cargo. NATO has now adopted standard pallets which measure 1,000 mm wide, 1,200 mm long and 1,370 mm or 1,575 mm high.

Fig. 23 M 109 Ammunition carrier

Palletisation demands vehicles which have flat load carrying 'beds' which conform to pallet sizes and can be loaded from both sides. The beds are measured in multiples of pallets. The greater number of pallets a vehicle can carry the better, but the need for mobility often cuts down the load capability whether it is in pallets or otherwise. For some loads, and artillery ammunition is a good example, it is best if the pallets can be carried straight to the user. In other cases, and here company sized combat teams (CT) are the obvious example, mixed loads of smaller quantities are necessary: it is normally these which require a HMLC capability. Whenever a load must be transferred to a higher mobility vehicle, or broken down into mixed loads, time is lost and manpower is increased; mechanical load handling devices can save both.

Handling Devices

Fork lift trucks are essential for pallet handling in base depots and where hard standing is available. The British Army also has a fork lift, with a cross-country capability and a speed which enables it to keep up with convoys. It is named the Eager Beaver and is to be found where loads are transferred, at bridge sites and even as far forward as gun sites.

Another essential device for handling pallets is some form of lifting system on the vehicle. The British Army uses Crane Attachment Lorry Mounted (CALM) positioned either front, middle or rear of the cargo bed. It is unlikely they are needed on LMLCs which will not stray far from areas where fork lift trucks are available, but they are required on approximately 25% of MMLCs. Their disadvantage is that they take up room and reduce the load carrying capacity of the vehicle by 1.5 to 2 tonnes.

Replenishment Techniques

The make up of the logistic fleet and its peripheral handling equipment depends much on the terrain in which it operates and the method of replenishment used by combat teams and artillery batteries. In undeveloped areas MMLCs will be required to carry broken bulk loads for long distances on poor tracks, but in Central Europe in a mechanised warfare scenario and with a comprehensive network of roads to run on, the requirement depends much on the method of operation of the combat teams.

Fig. 24 British 8 tonnes MMLC

Until a few years ago, the use of jerrycans for all liquid replenishment tended to
rule forward replenishment thinking. It may now be time to review the necessity
to replenish AFVs in their tactical positions. It is most unlikely that an AFV will
survive so long in one position that it will use up sufficient ammunition to require
replenishment; it is equally unlikely to require fuel or food. It may, therefore,
be possible to devise a system whereby replenishment normally takes place when
the unit is moving and can move through a point where the logistic vehicles can
re-fuel them using tankers, replenish their ammunition from pallet loads and
water them from water bowsers. The Israeli Merkava tank has a door at the rear
which makes fast replenishment easy: perhaps this idea may be developed to allow
a pallet to be put in it? If replenishment in tactical positions, off roads, is the
exception, then the requirement for a HMLC may be small. If, however, the
armour and the infantry are convinced that replenishment is necessary in or near
tactical positions, then many more HMLCs will be required.

Further back along the logistic chain, it has often been mooted that trailers pulled
by other lorries, or the articulated trailer and tractor so common in the civilian
cargo business, should be used. The attraction of such a system is that trailers
can be left loaded to be picked up quickly when required. The arguments against
this are the cost of the large number of trailers required and their lack of man-
oeuvrability on poor tracks. A half way system which allows stores to be left
loaded is the Ampliroll which is illustrated in Fig. 25. It consists of a 'bed'
which can be winched on and off a lorry; the bed can be loaded or unloaded. It is
being tried out by the British Army.

Fig. 25 The Ampliroll system

Summary

There is no doubt that modern systems of cargo handling and movement have caused, and are still causing, military logisticians and tactical commanders to review their logistic operating methods. Improvements in road standards, road network coverage and civilian vehicles also cause further review. An important feature of the military logistic systems of the future is that they are organised to take advantage of advances in civilian cargo handling and road communications.

GAP CROSSING

Fig. 26 Chieftain bridge layer

Very closely connected with the overall mobility of mechanised forces is their ability to cross dry or wet gaps. Perhaps the most simple method devised is the fascine which is a roll of chestnut palings which can be dropped into a gap and provides a rough crossing. In the British Army fascines are carried on the Armoured Vehicle Royal Engineers (AVRE), but for particular operations they could be carried on MBTs. Some research has been carried out on inflatable fascines which are rather large rubber cylinders which can be inflated quickly by gas. Plastic tubes bundled together in fascines are now being introduced. The use of such a simple device to cross a small gap is not to be underestimated when it is realised that about 90% of gaps in Central Europe are less than 15 m wide.

Another quick assault bridge system used by most armies with tank formations is
that launched from a specially adapted tank chassis. The British Army version
of it is the Chieftain Armoured Vehicle Launched Bridge (AVLB) which spans
23 m with a class 60 bridge: it takes less than 5 minutes to lay. The West
German Army has a bridge layer mounted on a Leopard chassis.

Armies have developed different methods and equipment for crossing rivers. The
Russian Army has specialised units to construct its PMP bridge: it requires pon-
toons to support decks and tugs to keep it in place. The West German and British
Armies have the Amphibious Bridge M2 which can be used as a ferry or linked together as a bridge: its construction times are very fast and 60 m of Class 60
bridge is possible in 30 minutes. Fig. 27 shows the M2. In addition the British
Army has its Medium Girder Bridge (MGB) which can be built by a Royal Engineer
troop. It is made from a sectionalised kit: a 9.8 m span kit can be carried on two
lorries and trailers and be constructed in 30 minutes.

Fig. 27 M2 opened out and entering the water

An army's ability to cross gaps is an important factor in determining its mobility.
It exerts an influence on the design of vehicles, and in turn its design is controlled
by the vehicles it must carry across gaps. It will affect a commander's tactical
plans, particularly in Central Europe, where there are so many gaps.

COMPROMISES

If there were no manpower or financial restraints, it would be easy to plan a mechanised force with sufficient anti-tank gun vehicles, tanks, MICVs, a variety of recce vehicles and logistic vehicles to support them. It is how to make the best use of manpower and financial resources which is the problem. In this chapter we have looked at some of the options: only a good assessment of the terrain and a clear concept of operations will allow the best use to be made of the resources and there will always be a multiplicity of solutions. Soldiers, who are aware of all the implications, will be needed to state their clear requirement to the designers who will then design to the necessary compromises.

SELF TEST QUESTIONS

Question 1   What are the three main design characteristics which must
be balanced in a well designed tank?

Answer   . . . .

. . . .

. . . .

Question 2   What limits:
a   The maximum dimensions of a tank?

Answer   . . . .

b   The maximum weight of a tank?

Answer   . . . .

Question 3   What is the difference between battlefield mobility and tactical
mobility?

Answer   . . . .

. . . .

. . . .

. . . .

. . . .

Question 4   Give three factors in AFV design which affect mobility.

Answer   . . . .

. . . .

. . . .

Question 5   What are the main advantages and disadvantages of a smooth bore
tank gun compared with a rifled gun?

Advantages   . . . .

. . . .

. . . .

....

....

....

Disadvantages ....

....

Question 6   With what armament can armed helicopters currently be equipped?

Answer   ....

....

....

Question 7   What additional capabilities are required by a MICV as compared
with an APC?

Answer   ....

....

....

....

Question 8   What characteristics are required in a reconnaissance vehicle?
In what order of importance would you put them?

Answer   ....

....

....

....

....

Question 9   What are the three main characteristics required of load carrying
vehicles?

Answer   ....

....

....

Question 10   What methods are currently in service in European Armies to
              bridge gaps quickly?

              Answer   . . . .

                        . . . .

                        . . . .

                        . . . .

                        . . . .

                        . . . .

ANSWERS ON PAGE 175

2
Guns, Mortars and Rockets

INTRODUCTION

Artillery systems can be classified into two main groups: they are indirect fire and air defence systems. This chapter will cover indirect systems only, because much of the air defence systems are guided weapons which are dealt with in Chapter 8. For a more comprehensive study of artillery systems, Volumes 2 and 8 of this series are recommended.

INDIRECT FIRE SYSTEMS

The Role

Historically, pin point accuracy has been left to direct fire weapons such as tank or anti-tank guns, firing over limited ranges, with a direct line of sight between gun and target, at ranges of no more than 2,000 to 3,000 metres. Indirect fire systems have been, and still are used to provide neutralising, or suppressive, fire. They fire up to ranges of forty or fifty kilometres and although pin point accuracy is not possible or demanded, sufficient accuracy to hit Piccadilly Circus from approximately twenty-five kilometres away is required. The considerable range of indirect fire weapons can be used in two ways: to reach well into enemy held territory and to cover a wide frontage of friendly positions. The longer the range, the greater is the area which can be covered and the more use can be made of that great characteristic of indirect fire - flexibility: and more targets can be engaged more quickly by concentrating the fire of more guns. To ensure that targets can be quickly and effectively engaged involves a well integrated and controlled system comprising many elements.

The Elements of an Indirect Fire System

The first requirement of any indirect fire system is an accurate method of survey to ensure that guns' positions can be fixed with an accuracy of a few metres. In the past this has been achieved by surveying the guns in by traditional survey method. Today, modern artillery batteries have navigation systems, the British version is Position and Azimuth Determining System (PADS) which gives its position co-ordinates to an accuracy of 10 m.

Having fixed the guns' positions it is necessary to do the same for the Observation Post (OP) where the Forward Observation Officer (FOO) is: PADS is used once more. Now the system has two fixed points from which to work and by triangulation it is possible to work out the position of a target if the FOO can determine the distance and angle from his OP. He does so by using a Laser Range Finder (LRF) and a compass.

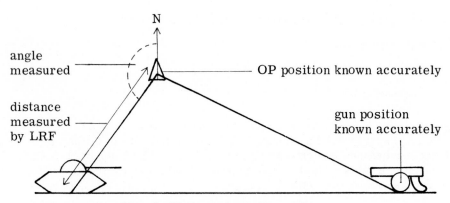

Fig. 1 Fixing a target's position

In the past the calculations have been made with the aid of a plotter board and slide rule. Now computers are used and the British Army, for example, uses the Field Artillery Computing Equipment (FACE). However, a computer can only produce effective gun data if it is fed with accurate facts.

We have seen how the target position is fixed in relation to that of the guns but the meteorological effects on the flight of the shell must be taken into account if a shell, which may travel to distances of over thirty kilometres and up to 8,000 metres in height, is to have any reasonable chance of hitting the target. The main effects are wind direction and speed, air pressure and air temperature. Another computer in service in the British Army, the Artillery Meteorology System (AMETS) is fed with the information from a sonde which is released into the atmosphere suspended from a balloon. After processing the information, AMETS presents it to FACE. FACE is then able to incorporate the information fed to it with the target and gun position details to provide accurate gun data.

Accurate data and accurate calculations are essential if guns are to land their first salvo on the target. This is a most important requirement. An enemy who sees that guns are ranging in on him is able to take good cover: it is the surprise of a sudden salvo on troops, who are not under cover, which is the most effective element of an artillery attack. It has been estimated that the effect of the first salvo from guns, landing on infantry in the open with no prior ranging, is five or six times as great as subsequent rounds.

Another essential element of an artillery system is good communications. A swift sure link which can work even in conditions of electronic warfare is required. Communications are dealt with in Chapter 6 of this book and in Volume 6 of this series.

It is important that a balance is kept in developing an artillery system. It is not much use producing a rocket or gun which can reach well into enemy territory unless there is a surveillance device which can see far enough to acquire the target. Nor is a superbly accurate gun, linked with a high definition surveillance device effective without reliable, quick reacting communications and an accurate method of calculating gun data. Indeed it is interesting to ponder which single improvement to the system will produce the greatest increase in effectiveness. Other parts of the system will be studied in other chapters but the basic element, which is the gun, mortar or rocket used to launch the ammunition which does the damage, will be covered in this chapter. Mortars, which are the most simple, are dealt with first.

MORTARS

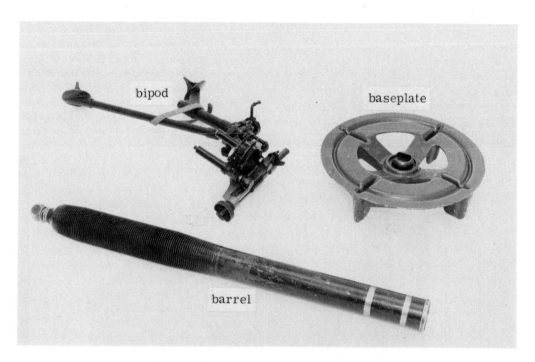

Fig. 2 The components of a mortar

Mortars have not been widely used in the British Army, but European armies have made extensive use of them. Their main advantages are they are simple, cheap and fire a very effective projectile. They are also light compared with guns and can be broken into three man portable parts: these are the tube or barrel, the base plate and the bipod. It must be remembered, however, that someone is also

required to carry ammunition! Despite its simplicity a mortar can produce a
very high rate of fire.

The simplicity is derived from its lack of a recoil system. Except for some of
the more complicated designs, the ground is used to take the recoil. Because of
this, the mortar is fired in the upper register (above 800 mil) only, and its relative inaccuracy, as compared with a gun, stems a great deal from its bomb's consequent long and high flight. Having said that, modern mortars are now able to
achieve a beaten zone almost comparable with that of a gun. For example the
81 mm British mortar will drop 50% of its bombs in an area 60 metres long by
30 metres wide at a range of over 5,000 metres. This compares with the British
Light Gun's ability to drop 50% of its 105 mm shells into an area 50 metres long
by 34 metres wide at over 17,000 metres.

Fig. 3 British 81 mm Mortar bomb

Most mortars have a short range
because the bomb is designed to
travel slower than the speed of
sound. From Fig. 3 it can be seen
that the 81 mm mortar bomb is fin
stabilised and has a shape which is
suited to good fragmentation as it
lands at a steep angle. (In Chapter
3 it is explained a little more why a
mortar bomb is such a good fragmenting projectile.) If a bomb were
to be designed to travel faster than
sound, compromises would be
necessary. First, the forces within
the mortar barrel would be greater,
which would necessitate a thicker
case for the bomb. This would ren-
der it less lethal because the fragmentation would be less effective
(see Chapter 3). Secondly, the
sound barrier shock wave would be
set up as shown in Fig. 4, which
would force the air flow wide of the
tail, making very long fins necessary to stabilise the bomb. In addition better streamlining of the bomb
would be necessary. Large fins
would need to be folded or alternat-
ively a sub-calibre bomb, with discarding sabots, would be required.
Streamlining would again reduce the
fragmenting efficiency of the bomb
because the shape would not be so
suitable.

In addition to the compromises
which affect the bomb, a stronger

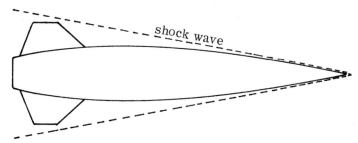

Fig. 4 Problem of supersonic mortar bomb

barrel would be necessary with a complementary increase in weight. In the end
any increase in range achieved by an increase in muzzle velocity would be at the
expense of simplicity, weight and lethality.

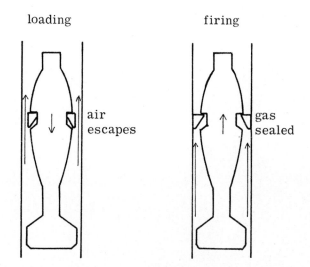

Fig. 5 Solution of mortar bomb windage problem

A basic problem with mortars has always been that of "windage". When a mortar
bomb is dropped down the barrel there must be an air gap around the bomb, otherwise it will stick or drop very slowly, so slowing down the rate of fire. However,
on the way up the barrel a good seal is required so that the propellant gases cannot escape, so causing a reduction in muzzle velocity and range. Attempts to
solve the problem have involved the use of an air valve at the bottom of the barrel
to allow air out as the bomb dropped, but the valve was subject to fouling and
sticking. Another method was to use breech loading mortars, but these spoiled
the simplicity of the mortar concept. In the end the development of a plastic
sealing ring which the propellant gases expand against the barrel walls has provided the solution on the British 81 mm mortar. The problem and the solution is
illustrated in Fig. 5.

Mortars are of great value where simplicity, area coverage, lethality, high rate of fire and the saving of manpower are important and a short range is acceptable. They were, in times past, often the only available weapon able to engage enemy troops behind crests, but now most modern guns are designed to fire in the upper and lower register and can carry out most mortar tasks with greater accuracy and at a greater range, but, at the expence of complexity, more manpower, greater weight, slower rate of fire and greater cost. However, because the projectile travels faster and normally not at such a high angle, guns can not be so easily located by radar.

GUNS

Fig. 6 British 105 mm light gun

Towed Guns

Until the end of the 1939-45 war, indirect fire guns were towed. Over the years
their weights have been reduced and the ranges increased, until today a gun firing
a 105 mm shell to a range of approximately seventeen kilometres, such as the
British light gun, can be towed behind a landrover.

Sweden has now developed its FH 77 towed gun and a consortium of Germany,
Italy and the United Kingdom has developed the FH 70. Both have a bore of 155
mm; both can fire to a range of twenty-four kilometres and methods are being
developed to extend this to thirty kilometres. To understand what improvements
are possible and the implications involved it is important first to look at the make-
up of a gun.

A Gun's Components

The basic components of a typical towed gun can be seen in Fig. 7.

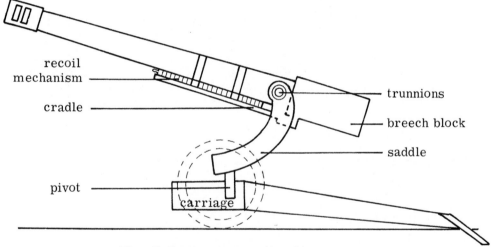

Fig. 7 Basic components of a towed gun

The barrel and breech are referred to jointly as the ordnance and rest in the
cradle which allows the ordnance to slide backwards and forwards when it recoils.
The recoil system's function is to smooth the backward movement of the ordnance
when it is being fired and return it smoothly to its original position. It performs
the same damping function as the suspension of a car.

The saddle forms a pivot on which the ordnance, recoil system and the cradle can
traverse: it also embodies other pivots, known as trunnions, which allow the vertical movement of the same components. The saddle rotates on the carriage or
mounting; the difference between the two is that the term carriage is used when
the gun fires with its wheels in contact with the ground; mounting is used when
wheels are not in contact with the ground during firing. Fig. 8 shows a

photograph of FH 70 on its carriage.

Fig. 8 FH 70 showing carriage

A trail is required to transmit firing stresses to the ground and is also used in
most guns to connect to the towing vehicle.

Self Propelled (SP) Guns

There has been, amongst Warsaw Pact and NATO nations in particular, a move
towards SP guns during the past two decades. At first the tremendous increase
in the cost of the equipment, and the danger of losing the use of a gun because of
automotive failure, would appear to cast doubt on the cost effectiveness of a SP
gun. However there are many advantages to be gained. Perhaps one of the most
important is the capability to carry on firing under counter bombardment; such an
ability would be much appreciated by the infantry relying on Final Protective Fire
(FPF) from their supporting artillery. A SP gun is also quicker to move to avoid
counter bombardment and, because of its tracks, has a better cross-country performance than towed guns. When it arrives in its new position it can come into
action very quickly because it has several rounds ready stowed in the vehicle. It
can, too, if fitted with collective NBC, carry on firing under NBC conditions or
traverse contaminated areas. Finally, because of the readily available vehicle
power, automatic ramming can be installed to permit a fast burst rate of fire.
The importance of this capability is covered later in this chapter.

Examples of SP guns are the widely used United States equipment M 109, which is shown in Fig. 9, and the USSR's M 1973, 152 mm gun. At a smaller level there is the British 105 mm Abbot and the USSR's M 1974, 122 mm.

Fig. 9 The 155 mm M 109 SP gun

Unlike the larger guns both these have a swimming capability. The stability of a SP gun is good, provided that the AFV design of the whole equipment, which is covered in Chapter 1, is sound.

Whether guns are towed or SP, factors which affect their effectiveness, such as shell lethality, accuracy, range, overall rate of fire and the burst rate of fire are the same. These are worth closer study.

Lethality of Shells

The fragmentation effectiveness of shells is dealt with more fully in Chapter 3. In this chapter it is only necessary to discuss their size and general capabilities. If the requirement were to attack infantry in the open there would be a good case for many small shells giving an even area coverage of shrapnel over an area. However, the requirement is more complex, including the disruption of armoured attacks and the neutralisation of troops dug in or in buildings, for which large shells are much more suitable. Because of the preponderance of armoured forces the tendency in Europe is to move to relatively large shells of 152 mm or 155 mm size. The weight comparison between the 105 mm and a 155 mm shell is

35 lbs to 96 lbs.

Fig. 10 Comparison of 105
mm and 155 mm shell size

The smaller shell is unlikely to disrupt an
attack made in armoured vehicles, whereas
heavy concentrations of 152 mm or 155 mm
shells may well do so. A 155 mm shell
which bursts near all but the better armoured APCs or Mechanised Infantry Combat
Vehicles (MICVs), if its fragmentation is
well designed, may defeat the armour of
those vehicles and cause casualties amongst
the crew. On the other hand, unless a
direct hit is scored, it is most unlikely
that a tank would be destroyed, but near
bursts would cause damage to optics,
antennas and external equipment, in addition to demoralising the crew. Larger
shells still, like the 175 mm or 8 inch guns,
can be even more effective against protected targets, but the equipments are very
large and there is a trend, of long standing
in the Warsaw Pact, to favour rockets instead of such large calibre guns. Rockets
are dealt with later in this chapter. A gun,
however, still remains supreme, when
compared with mortars and rockets, when
accuracy is required.

Accuracy of Guns

Most soldiers understand the difference,
when applied to small arms, between
grouping and accuracy. After a small
group has been consistently obtained it is
possible, by adjusting the sights of the
weapon, to apply that small consistent
grouping to the centre of the target to
achieve accuracy. The same processes
apply to artillery systems. Consistency,
which takes the place of grouping, demands that ammunition does not vary from
round to round: this, in its turn, rests on the consistent performance of the propellant and the uniform manufacture of the projectiles. It also demands the gun's
performance does not vary from round to round: to achieve this, it is necessary
that the gun returns to exactly the same position after each firing and that the
barrel which "whips" when it fires, "whips" in the same way each time. Then
there are such factors as precise surveying, precise measurements by FOOs,
well found meteorological data and exact calculations which we have discussed
before, all of which contribute to consistency. The consistency achieved by the
105 mm Abbot gun is such that 50% of its rounds will fall in an area 7 metres
wide and 64 metres long at over 17 kilometres, which means that it could drop

50% of its shells well within the Serpentine lake in Hyde Park, firing from the runway of Heathrow Airport. To apply the consistent fire of a gun is merely a matter of good gun sighting no matter what the range is.

Range of Guns

Unless there is an observation and target acquisition system which can look well into enemy held territory, the main advantage of long range is the flexibility to be gained from the coverage of the wide front. In general terms, the range of a gun can be improved by increasing the muzzle velocity or boosting the projectile whilst it is in flight or improving the projectile's ballistic performance.

Increased muzzle velocity can be achieved in various ways: one of the most obvious, perhaps, is to have a longer barrel, so that the propellant gases have a longer time in which to push and accelerate the projectile. A longer heavier barrel, however, demands larger recoil mechanisms and an altogether heavier gun. Another method is to make shells with more propellant, so producing a greater propellant gas pressure, but this also results in a heavier barrel because of the greater strength required. Improvements in materials may result in lighter, stronger metals which may compensate, but probably the limit has been reached for now.

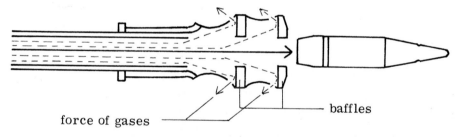

force of gases ——————————————————— baffles

Fig. 11 Action of muzzle break

One way to alleviate the forces on the recoil system and reduce the weight on the gun for a given muzzle velocity, is to add a muzzle brake; they can be seen on the FH 70 and the Light Gun. They deflect, to the side and rear, some of the propellant gases after the projectile has left the gun. As the gases press on the back face of the baffles (see Fig. 11) so the recoil of the barrel is slowed and less stress is transmitted to the recoil system. However, rarely is an advantage gained without paying for it, and so it is with muzzle brakes. If they are to be made very effective then the noise, which is deflected back to the gun crews, is too much and damages their ears.

Boosting the projectile in flight can result in considerable range increases: it is estimated that a Rocket Assisted Projectile (RAP) could increase the range of a modern 155 mm gun by approximately six kilometres. However the rocket booster would take up some 20% to 30% of the HE's place in the projectile and so reduce its lethality. (See Fig. 12).

A system called Base Bleed, which fills the vacuum behind the projectile with a slowly released gas, has recently shown promise. When the vacuum is filled, the drag on the projectile is reduced. (See Fig. 12). It may take up approximately 10% of the HE's space which is not so much as in the RAP's case, but it is not known yet whether the range increase will be so dramatic.

rocket motor   HE   gas   HE

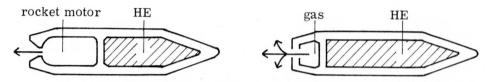

Fig. 12 Illustration of RAP and Base Bleed shells

Greater ranges have also been achieved by improving the streamlining of shells to give them better aerodynamic and ballistic characteristics. Unfortunately the streamlining narrows the shell, leaves less space for HE and so reduces its lethality.

The deductions are that range can be increased, but unless lighter, stronger and more costly materials are used, the trade off is heavier guns, deaf gunners or less lethality. The relative merits of greater range against these disadvantages is for the soldier to decide upon.

Overall Rate of Fire of Guns

The rates of fire of guns are limited by overheating and the size and weight of the rounds. Some rapid firing air defence guns have been water cooled, but for other uses, unless the user is willing to accept the complication which would arise when guns are water cooled, little can be done beyond making barrels thicker, so being able to absorb and conduct away the heat. So the rate of fire of guns is, in theory, often limited by overheating. In fact, tactics and the logistics of ammunition supply would normally provide the real limitations on rates of fire.

Tank guns often experience heating problems. Their high muzzle velocity and consequent high gas pressures cause rapid heating and then, especially when there is a wind, rapid cooling occurs on one side. As a result the barrel bends. The solution is to wrap the barrel in a thermal jacket, which explains the Chieftain tank gun's overcoat.

A heavy round is another limiting factor, which again is well illustrated in the case of the Chieftain. It has a large 120 mm round and, although there are others, one of the main reasons for separating the propellant from the projectile is the difficulty of handling such a large and heavy piece of ammunition in a restricted space. The same argument is amplified when applied to the 155 mm indirect fire guns. The total weight of a 155 mm round is in the region of 45 kg (100 lbs) which is too heavy to be handled and rammed up into the breech quickly. It is also split into its projectile and propellant parts, which can then be handled separately; but as two separate items must be loaded each time the gun fires, the rate of loading and firing is slower than when fixed ammunition is used. For a sustained rate of fire, which is normally one or two rounds per minute, it is not a major limitation; but a burst rate of fire demands that a few rounds are fired at intervals of three or four seconds and here is a major problem.

Burst Rate of Fire of Guns

Fig. 13 Swedish FH 77 with a mechanical loader and rammer

The effectiveness of putting down a first salvo on the target, while the enemy is unprepared, was stressed earlier in this chapter. This idea can be extended to the provision of a sudden flurry of salvos on the target rather than a long slow series of them. This concept is now known as the burst rate of fire. A gunner asks for, and the designer attempts to provide, the ability to land a rapid series of rounds, from each gun, on the target. Currently the asking rate is approximately 3 rounds in 8 to 12 seconds. This can only be achieved with 155 mm guns if some form of mechanical assistance is given to the gunner loading the gun. Mechanical rammers have often been used before on heavy guns. They are most needed in a SP gun, where cramped conditions make rammed handling difficult, and fortunately on such equipment the power is readily available. Nevertheless they are still required on towed guns if burst rates of fire are required. Modern towed guns such as FH 70 or the Swedish FH 77 have small engines to allow limited motoring without the towing vehicles and a power take-off is possible.

The Swedish have produced a prototype of a mechanical loader and rammer. This
is shown in Fig. 13.

A sudden heavy concentration from several batteries of guns, with a high burst
rate of fire capability, is very effective. It needs a high degree of control which
will be considered later in this chapter, but perhaps an even better way to produce such a demoralising weight of fire on a concentration of enemy forces is to
use rockets.

ROCKETS

Fig. 14 USSR 122 mm BM 21 MLRS

Rockets have been used in war for much longer than guns. Their origin goes
back to China but their heyday was in the 18th and 19th centuries when muzzle
loading cannon had a slow rate of fire, were inaccurate and were short on range.
It was not until the skills which were developed during the industrial revolution
became available that the manufacture of accurate guns became possible; after
that rockets reverted to being a shock weapon when a very heavy weight of fire
was necessary. They were used at D Day landings, the Germans in the 1939 -
45 war had their Nebelwerfer and the Russians had their Stalin Organs which
created such demoralising effects on their foes. The Warsaw Pact have continued
to field Multi Launch Rocket Systems (MLRS) such as the 122 mm BM 21 shown
in Fig. 14. A battalion of 18 BM 21 can produce 30,000 lbs of HE on to a target
in 20 seconds. It would take approximately 320 rounds of 155 mm to do this.

Even using guns able to fire four rounds each in 20 seconds, it would take approximately 80 guns to equal such a concentration of fire.

To understand the advantages and disadvantages of a rocket it is necessary to
understand its basic elements.

nozzle   fins   propellant   warhead   fuze and nose cap

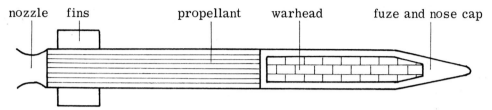

Fig. 15 Basic components of a free flight rocket (FFR)

Because it carries its own propellant with it, a rocket does not need a gun to
launch it on its way. Consequently a light weight launching system is possible,
such as the BM 21; but the actual round of ammunition is much larger than a
shell, so the logistic load is much greater. Rapid launching of rockets also
throws up dust and smoke, so the launch signature is easily detectable. Because
the rocket motor travels with the warhead, a greater weight of projectile than is
the case with a shell must be accelerated away: this requires the use of a large
amount of propellant and a slower launch rate. However the slow launch rate has
advantages: the warhead is not subject to such firing stresses as a shell. It is
this factor which permits the warhead to be more readily designed for its effect
when it lands than is possible with a shell. The fragmentation can be controlled
by notching. Even more effective against APCs and MICVs would be a wall of
ball bearings around the warhead. For tank attack, bomblets such as those shown
in Fig. 15 in Chapter 3 or minelets could be used: and in the next section more
advanced warheads are considered.

The two drawbacks to rockets are relatively poor accuracy and difficulty in adjusting the range. The accuracy problem is partly caused by side winds on the
fins of the slow flying rockets and partly by the difficulty of manufacturing rocket
motors and nozzles which can produce consistent performances to control rockets
to accuracies of 50 - 100 metres at about 40 km range. Nevertheless, over the
past two decades, advances have been made to produce accuracies beginning to
compare with those of modern guns.

Rockets can probably replace most heavy guns and provide a more immediately
devastating demoralising effect than is possible with guns: but the logistic load
is a big disadvantage.

IMPROVED MUNITIONS

It has been the dream of most gunners to have the capability of attacking armour
with indirect fire. The development of sub-munitions has brought about some
ability to do so and bomblets, similar to those described in Chapter 3, can be
effective against the top armour of tanks.

The next stage now being considered is to use a Cannon Launched Guided Projectile (CLGP). In its current form, the United States Copperhead, it is launched from a 155 mm indirect fire gun and guided on to its target by a FOO using a laser designator (see Chapter 7, Fig. 9). This is a big step forward, but there are drawbacks. The first is that the target must be in line of sight from the FOO and stay in sight during the time taken to give fire orders, launch the CLGP and then allow it to cover the distance from the gun to the target. Secondly, low cloud cover may obscure the laser designation signal from the projectile until it is too late to correct its course.

In the future, micro-electronics may allow sub-munitions to contain their own seeker heads. They could be ejected from their carrier warheads over the target area and seek out their own individual targets. An example of this concept is SADARM (Seek And Destroy ARMour) which is being studied in the United States and is illustrated in Fig. 16. If such a concept could be translated into hardware, it might have a revolutionary effect on the tactics of mechanised battles.

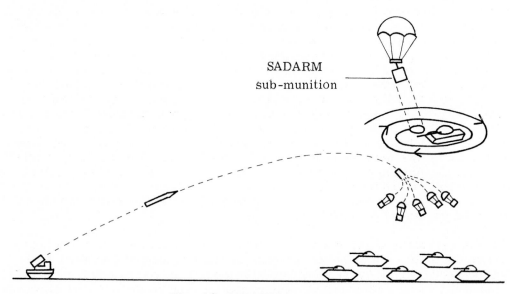

SADARM
sub-munition

Fig. 16 SADARM concept

FAMILY OF INDIRECT WEAPONS

An ideal indirect fire system employs a mixture of mortars with varying sizes of guns and rockets to carry out the role required of the artillery. At the beginning of this chapter, that role was defined as a necessity to neutralise enemy forces. Within that overall role there are several refinements. Perhaps one of the most demanding is to provide the close fire support (CFS) as close as possible to friendly armour and infantry either in the attack or defence. As a measure, a 105 mm gun can bring fire down to within 250 metres of infantry in the open, a 81 mm mortar can do the same, whereas a 155 mm gun would need another 100 metres, and a 175 mm gun would need nearly three times the distance of the 105 mm. A rocket system could not be used in this role. It can be seen from these figures that a medium mortar can be used for CFS but its large area coverage renders it not so effective as a light gun. On the other hand mortars can produce a heavy weight of fire quickly, economically, and they are very good at producing harrassing and neutralising fire at short ranges, especially in the attack. They can also produce defensive fire, but for Final Protective Fire (FPF) missions a light gun would be best.

For Depth Fire Support (DFS), rocket and heavy guns are the queens of the battlefield. Heavy guns are more effective against dug in troops protected in buildings while rockets can provide a more immediate devastating effect. Airportability is an important requirement for guns to be used in difficult terrain such as the Arctic, mountainous country, swampy or jungle areas; especially desirable is the capability to be carried in or under a helicopter: mortars and towed light guns are the answer. In central European or desert warfare, SP guns with a calibre of 155 mm and rockets capable of disrupting armoured forces hold dominance.

Every tactician, especially if he is a gunner, holds his own views on what is the optimum mix for each set of circumstances, but the trends which will produce an effective indirect fire system for particular theatres are there to be seen by any soldier.

CONTROL OF INDIRECT FIRE SYSTEMS

To extract the maximum effect from an indirect fire system, there must be a method of control which can provide an assessment of priorities and the application of good judgement. A slight understanding of computers, which are covered partly in Chapter 6 and much more in Volumes 2 and 6 of this series, reveals that they could be a considerable aid. To date, control has been vested entirely in the hands of the normal command structure, with a good measure of it in the hands of the FOO. Computers have been introduced first to compute gun data (eg FACE) and meteorological data (eg AMETS). In the future a wider use of them is being considered.

A computer system could be fed with information covering the location of each battery and its ammunition stocks, then to that could be added the locations and types of targets as they arise. If the computer were suitably programmed for the task then it would be possible for it to allot the targets to batteries and arrange them into an order of priority; then it could calculate how many rounds, of what nature and at which rate, should be fired. The level at which this collation and ordering of information should be carried out is a matter for careful consideration. For economy and overall efficiency of artillery effort, the higher the control the better, but this may weaken the intimate relationship between gunners and the units they support with a consequent reduction in trust. No computer programmer can foresee every situation which may arise, so there must be, at artillery divisional or brigade or regimental level, a gunner who can override the computer assessment; again the best level for this override capability must be considered carefully.

There is an obvious important role for computers in indirect fire systems and they could provide an invaluable aid to control in a future fast moving conflict in which there would be a multitude of targets. They can only be regarded as an

aid, however, and they must be linked by reliable communications which can work
through enemy electronic warfare measures.

DIRECT FIRE GUNS

Conventional Guns

Whereas the primary role of indirect fire guns is to neutralise, direct fire guns
have a primary role which is to destroy point targets, with an emphasis on AFVs
and aircraft. This chapter will deal with guns primarily designed to defeat AFVs;
air defence guns, which are mainly cannons, are covered in Chapter 5.

The mechanisms by which the projectiles defeat armour are dealt with in Chapter
3 under the heading of ammunition. Guns which fire brute force kinetic energy
rounds such as the APDS and APFSDS rounds (see Chapter 3) need to pack as
much punch as possible into the projectile before it leaves the gun's muzzle;
which means it must leave that muzzle with as high a velocity as can be achieved;
so the gun must be able to withstand high stresses. A comparison between the
British 105 mm light gun and the British 105 mm tank gun will serve to bring out
the characteristics which are emphasised in a high pressure tank gun.

The tank gun is about one and one third the length of the light gun; this allows
more time for the propellant gases to push the projectile to high velocities. The
weight of the tank gun's barrel is over twice that of the light gun; this is partly
because of its length, but simple mathematics will show this is not the complete
answer. Part of the weight is caused by the thicker barrel which is necessary to
prevent the bending, caused by rapid heating and uneven cooling, described
earlier in this chapter; part is used to absorb some of the recoil, which must be
kept to a minimum in the confined space of a tank turret; and part is the additional
weight of the fume extractor, which is to be seen on tank guns and SP guns: the
object is to reduce, as much as possible, the fumes entering the enclosed vehicle
space when the breech is opened. Its method of operation can be seen in Fig. 17.

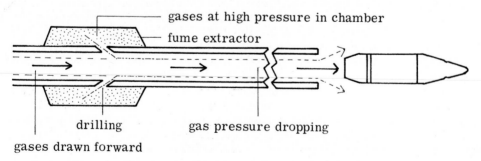

gases at high pressure in chamber

fume extractor

drilling   gas pressure dropping

gases drawn forward

Fig. 17 Operation of fume extractor

As the projectile passes the angled drillings, the high pressure gases are pushed
through them into the fume extractor chamber. When the projectile leaves the
muzzle, the gas pressure in the chamber causes a surge of gases forward through

the drillings towards the muzzle. This causes a flow from the breech to the muzzle thus drawing the fumes forward.

Guns which fire kinetic energy rounds can also fire HESH rounds and HEAT rounds at smaller muzzle velocities. If , however, light weight guns, for infantry use, are required to defeat modern tanks then there is no question of them attempting to use kinetic energy. In fact the only way to produce an effective light weight anti-tank gun in modern times is to do away with the need for a heavy barrel, breech and recoil system. This is a description of a recoilless gun (RCL).

Recoilless Gun

Fig. 18 British 120 mm Wombat recoilless gun

The essence of a recoilless gun is in the ammunition which is described in Chapter 3. The propellant gases are released to the air through a venturi at the rear of the barrel after sufficient pressure has been built up to force the projectile out of its cartridge case and down the barrel.

A RCL consists of a lightweight rifled tube with the venturi on the rear end, fitted on to a carriage to ease the tube's movement. A sighting system and a traversing and elevating system complete the equipment, which in the case of the British

120 mm Wombat pictured in Fig. 18, weighs less than a quarter tonne.

CHOICE OF IMPROVEMENTS

Guns, mortars , rockets and their ammunition are all steadily being improved in terms of range, lethality, accuracy and mobility; better surveillance and target acquisition devices are being developed and the rapid improvement in electronics based devices is manifesting itself in improved control and communications systems and may result in self seeking sub-munitions. The dilemma is to choose where, in the indirect fire system in particular, the limited resources can be best used to achieve the greatest advantage.

SELF TEST QUESTIONS

Question 1   What are the main elements of an indirect fire system?

Answer ....

....

....

....

....

....

....

Question 2   What are the advantages and disadvantages of a mortar compared with a gun?

Advantages ....

....

....

....

....

....

Disadvantages ....

....

....

....

Question 3   What advantages does a SP gun have over a towed gun?

Answer ....

....

....

....

....

....

Question 4   What methods are there of increasing the range of a gun?

Answer ....

....

....

....

....

....

Question 5   What is meant by 'burst rate of fire' and why is it important?

Answer ....

....

....

....

....

Question 6   If warhead lethality were the only criterion in what order would
you place mortars, guns and rockets to carry that warhead?
Give reasons for your choice.

a   ....

b   ....

c   ....

....

....

....

Question 7   What are the advantages and disadvantages of Free Flight Rockets?

Advantages ....

....

....

....

Disadvantages   ....

....

....

....

....

Question 8   What types of improved munitions have recently been introduced
              or are being studied?

              Answer ....

                      ....

                      ....

                      ....

Question 9   What functions in an artillery system could be carried out by
              computers in the future?

              Answer ....

                      ....

                      ....

                      ....

                      ....

                      ....

Question 10   In what ways is a tank gun likely to differ from a similar calibre
              indirect fire gun?

              Answer ....

                      ....

                      ....

ANSWERS ON PAGE 176

3
Ammunition
(Including Mines and Grenades)

SCOPE

The term ammunition covers a wide range of devices from pistol bullets to high velocity anti-tank projectiles, from grenades to heavy artillery shells and from simple illuminating rockets to intercontinental ballistic missiles. This chapter will deal with the outline design of cartridge systems which propel the projectile from the weapon and then the types of projectile which are used. It will also extend to rocket and guided weapon warheads but not their propellants which are considered comprehensively in Volume 8 of this series. A section on mines will also be included.

COMPLETE ROUNDS

The structure of the round is determined by the design of the weapon from which it is fired: the main categories which result are known as Quick Firing (QF), Recoilless (RCL) and Separate Case or Breech Loading (BL) systems. There are variations, but they can be treated as sub categories of these three. The propellant in the QF round is encased in a metal, which can be steel or brass. The case seals the breech end of the barrel to prevent any escape of gas: this action of sealing is called obturation. The projectile is gripped firmly in the neck of the case and the resultant complete round is loaded into the weapon in one piece: it is this single loading action which allows the "Quick Firing" of the weapon.

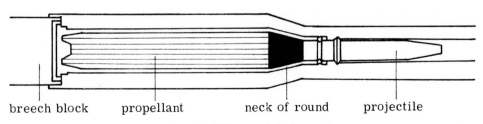

| breech block | propellant | neck of round | projectile |

Fig. 1 QF round in breech

When the propellant is ignited it burns. A gas pressure builds up and expands
the case to form a seal against the wall of the breech: in this way obturation is
achieved. As the gas pressure increases, it forces the projectile out of the neck,
along the barrel and out of the muzzle. When the gases follow the projectile out,
the pressure in the barrel and the case reduces. The case is no longer pushed
tightly against the walls of the breech and can be extracted.

A recoilless gun, as its name aptly describes, has no recoil and so has no need
of a buffer system. Consequently it is lighter than a conventional gun, but the
price paid for this advantage is a heavy RCL round, and, as will be explained, a
lower muzzle velocity. In Fig. 2 a RCL round is portrayed in its associated
weapon.

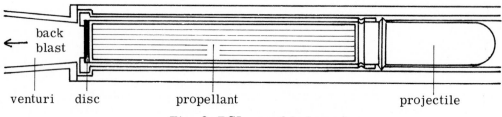

Fig. 2 RCL round in breech

When the propellant is ignited the gases produced begin to build up the pressure
as they do in a QF cartridge. The design principle which allows the RCL round
to operate successfully is in the balance between the restraining grip exerted by
the neck of the cartridge case on the projectile and the bursting limit of the disc
in the base of the cartridge. The projectile breaks away from the grip and begins
to move a few milliseconds before the disc bursts, after which the equal and
opposite forces push the projectile along the barrel one way and the gases through
the venturi in the other. The weapon remains still.

For guns using rounds which would be too large to be loaded in one piece, either
because their weight would preclude man handling or because their length would
cause stowage and mechanical handling difficulties, the solution is a Breech
Loading (BL) design. It is often, perhaps better, described as "separated
ammunition" because the projectile and propellant are separate from each other.
After the projectile has been rammed to the forward end of the breech the separate
propellant is pushed up behind it. In separated ammunition the propellant may be
contained in a combustible case with a metal stub base; or a very common system,
used in most artillery guns and the Chieftain tank gun, is to contain the propellant
in bags. With no case to effect the essential obturation, the breech must be carefully designed and manufactured to fulfil this role itself.

PROPELLANTS

The function of the cartridge charge, or propellant, is to burn very quickly to
produce rapidly expanding gases and a great pressure: this propels the projectile
down the barrel with a high acceleration. The main component of the charge is a

"low" explosive which burns rather than detonates instantaneously. Unfortunately for designers, a propellant of such characteristics is difficult to initiate and an explosive train is required leading from a small amount of easily detonated sensitive "high" explosive through progressively less sensitive intermediaries to the main propellant.

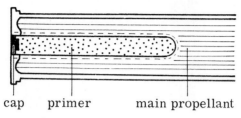

cap   primer   main propellant

Fig. 3 Explosive train in a cartridge

A typical cartridge explosive train is illustrated in Fig. 3. The cap can be initiated, depending on its design and composition, by a blow from a firing pin or by an electrical impulse. It produces a flash, which ignites the less sensitive explosive in the primer. In its turn, through ports in its containing tube, it ignites the least sensitive main propellant.

PROJECTILES

The other main element of a round of ammunition is the projectile. The simplest projectile of all is the small arms round.

Small Arms Round

Perhaps the easiest approach to the design of a small arms round is to consider its "stopping power". As a rough guide, a bullet must transfer 80 joules (59 ft lbf) of energy to a man to stop him and put him out of action. To achieve this, a projectile of sufficient weight must be given sufficient velocity for the distance over which the round is to be effective. As is explained in Chapter 5 and expanded upon in Volume 5 of this series, the trend is now to smaller projectiles than in the past, with higher velocities: the higher velocities compensate for the reduced stopping power which would otherwise result from the smaller bullets. The shape of the bullet in small arms, as in all projectiles, is a compromise between the need to do the maximum amount of damage when it arrives at its target and the need for it to get there, accurately, through the air. A flat-nosed bullet would do the most damage but a slim, pointed-nosed round is required to reach out to an adequate range with accuracy.

By far the most widely used small arms round is an anti-personnel projectile. It is called "ball". Two other types in common use are armour piercing (AP) and tracer. The general design of them is given on the next page in Fig. 4.

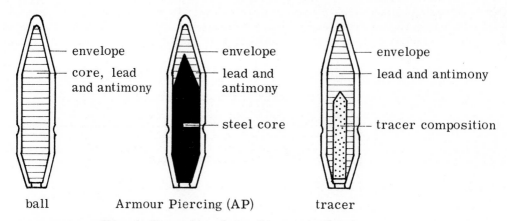

ball   Armour Piercing (AP)   tracer

Fig. 4 Examples of small arms bullet design

All rounds require an envelope which is strong enough to withstand the pressures of being fired. It must also be ductile to engage the rifling in the barrel: it is this which imparts the spin. Nickel, which causes little fouling, is commonly used. Inside the envelope the structure of the core is controlled by the need to penetrate the target and for the bullet to remain stable as it travels through the air. To achieve this the centre of gravity should be as near the base as possible to retain good stability, which in its turn helps to produce a good penetrating capability over a good range.

Fragmenting Projectiles

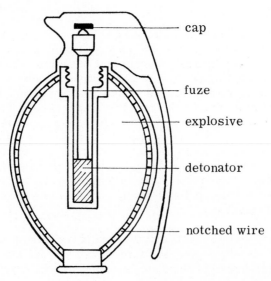

Fig. 5 The American M26 (or British L2A1) grenade using notched wire

The compromise between achieving the maximum effectiveness at the receiving end whilst being able to retain the ballistic performance to achieve a good range becomes more difficult with fragmenting projectiles. The easiest situation to design for is when the projectile is thrown by hand: this describes a grenade and the only real limitations are that it must be small enough to be held in the hand and light enough to be thrown.

For some years now it has been accepted that an effective anti-personnel device should produce fragments of approximately a gram. There is little problem in doing this because the wall of a grenade can be notched on its inside to ensure that this happens. A common way of doing it is to use a notched wire coil which is wound round the inside of a thin case. The American M26 grenade, also in service with the British Army as the L2A1, uses this design (see Fig. 5). The remainder of the grenade consists of an explosive train to blow the notched wire into its 1,250 fragments which the notching pre-determines.

After grenades, the easiest projectile to design is the warhead of a rocket or surface to surface guided weapon (SSGW). Such warheads are not subject to the extreme firing stresses experienced by shells in gun barrels. Because the acceleration of a rocket or a SSGW is relatively low, it is possible to fit an efficient fragmentation warhead which may have notched walls to permit optimum fragmentation or even a warhead envelope lined with ball bearings of a predetermined size. In general, however, rockets or SSGW are too expensive to carry relatively simple fragmentation devices and if they do not have a nuclear or chemical warhead the trend is to use them to carry sub-munitions, about which more will be said later.

A mortar bomb is still relatively easy to design because it is normally fired at subsonic speeds: consequently its walls can be thinner than those of a shell, though notching can only be applied to light mortar bombs of about 60 mm or less; beyond this size the firing stresses tend to be too great. Here it is convenient to introduce the concept of the "Charge to Mass Ratio". A rule of thumb method for determining the effectiveness of the fragmentation of an anti-personnel device, remembering that the designer tries to achieve the maximum number of fragments of approximately one gram, is that the more explosive there is, in relation to the mass of the wall of the device, the better. In the extreme, a small amount of explosive detonated within a thick container may just crack it into two, whilst a large amount in a very thin case would blow it into powder. In practice, it is very difficult to design a projectile with walls which are too thin.

Because of the relatively low firing stresses a mortar bomb can be designed with a much thinner wall than a shell, so it is inherently a better fragmenting projectile. Moreover, by virtue of the near vertical angle at which it strikes the ground, it spreads the fragments around efficiently in a rough circle. A shell, which lands at a shallower angle, loses many of its fragments into the ground. Fig. 6 illustrates this.

The most difficult fragmentating projectile to design is the shell fired from a
modern high velocity gun. A soldier demands that an artillery gun should fire a
shell to great ranges, which involves a
high acceleration in the barrel leading to
a high muzzle velocity; he also demands
that it should be accurate, which means
that it must have a good aerodynamic
shape and that it should be spun at a fast
rate. Such requirements mitigate against
a weak, thin wall; but modern designers,
by the use of better metals and improved
explosives, are constantly improving the
important charge to mass ratio.

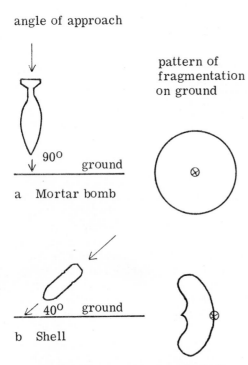

angle of approach

pattern of
fragmentation
on ground

90°   ground

a   Mortar bomb

40°   ground

b   Shell

Fig. 6 Mortar bomb and shell
fragmentation patterns

Anti-armour Projectiles

The necessity to compromise is equally
relevant to anti-armour projectiles.
Their main objective is to produce damage to the interior of armoured vehicles,
of which the tank is the most difficult
target to tackle. There are four main
approaches to achieving the necessary
behind armour effect. They are
normally classified firstly as kinetic
attack, secondly attack by High Explosive Squash Head (HESH) and known in the
United States as High Explosive Plastic
(HEP), thirdly attack by a charge most
often referred to as High Explosive Anti Tank (HEAT) and fourthly attack by a plate
charge. We will look at these in turn.

Kinetic Attack

Kinetic attack in concept is a brute force method. Basically it consists of hurling
as tough a piece of material as can be made, as fast as possible, against the
armour of a vehicle and so punching a hole in it. Once through the armour the
projectile, or often broken pieces of it, rattle around inside the vehicle and cause
damage. In fact the design of the projectiles and the development of the materials
used have become complicated. The first form of kinetic attack round was simply
a solid steel shell or shot known as an Armour Piercing (AP) round, but with
improvements in armour, both in materials and thickness, higher velocities were
required to achieve penetration. After a series of developments through the
1939 - 45 war and afterwards, the solid steel shot was developed into an Armour
Piercing Discarding Sabot (APDS) round, which was used in most western tank
guns. It is shown in simplified form in Fig. 7.

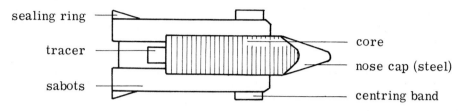

Fig. 7 Basic components of an APDS projectile

The design results from the conflicting requirements at each end of the projectile's flight. At the target end a thin penetrative slug of very dense material is required; while at the gun end a projectile with a wide base is necessary to produce a large area over which the pressure from the propellant gases can push to achieve the maximum thrust and muzzle velocity. The compromise in the APDS round is to enclose the slug, or more accurately the core, in a sabot which then permits a full gun bore base to be fitted. After the round leaves the barrel the sabot falls off leaving the core, with its nose cap, travelling towards the target. When it strikes, the nose cap which has a ballistic part to provide good aerodynamics and a piercing part to prevent the core shattering on impact, makes the first pene-tration: then the core drives through the armour to cause behind armour damage. Over recent years the core has often been made of tungsten carbide, but now depleted uranium is being considered by many nations.

To provide stability, the APDS round is spun and must be fired from a rifled gun. For a kinetic energy round there are limitations in this method, because the core cannot be made too long before it comes unstable: penetration of armour could be improved by making the core longer and thinner. This can be achieved by using fin stabilisation. It entails making the core into an arrow shape and firing it from a smooth bore barrel or arranging for a slipping driving band on the round which prevents it spinning as it goes down a rifled barrel. West Germany, USSR and the United States have opted for smooth bore guns whilst the United Kingdom has re-tained the rifled gun because it wishes to continue its use of the HESH round which can not easily be fin stabilised. An illustration of the major components of an Armour Piercing Fin Stabilised Discarding Sabot (APFSDS) round is at Fig. 8

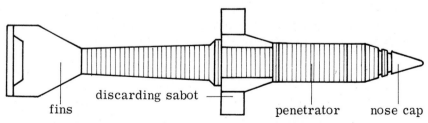

Fig. 8 Basic components of an APFSDS projectile

After the projectile has left the muzzle, the discarding sabot and the baseplate fall away and leave the graphically named long rod penetrator to carry on to the target, stabilised by its fins. Its advantages over the APDS round are that it has a higher muzzle velocity because it is fired from a smooth bore gun, and it achieves a greater penetration because it strikes the target with a smaller area backed up by a greater mass.

It can be readily seen that any kinetic energy projectile must be fired from a high pressure gun, which, almost by definition, means a long heavy gun on a big mounting. In fact it is normally mounted on a large armoured fighting vehicle. If smaller mountings are necessary for cost or concealment reasons, then other armour defeating methods must be used.

HESH Projectiles

By its very nature a HESH projectile can not be fired at very high velocity. The concept of a HESH warhead is simple, but like so many simple concepts it is not always easy to achieve, as was seen in the design of the kinetic energy rounds. The concept is that the warhead consists of, for a shell, a relatively large amount of plastic explosive. On arrival at the target the plastic explosive "cow pats" on the outside of the armour and is detonated by a fuze at its base. There is no attempt to penetrate the armour: instead a shock wave is set up in the armour which causes a scab of it to be blown off on the inside. The velocity of the scab is such that it rattles around inside the AFV and causes the behind armour damage.

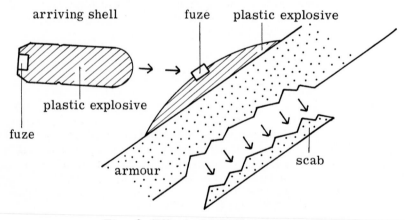

Fig. 9 Effect of HESH on armour

Because there is a considerable weight of explosive the secondary effects of the explosion are considerable; it is quite possible that vision devices would be cracked and radio antennas blown off; it would also be quite certain that the crew inside the vehicle would not feel like continuing their fighting for some time, if ever. Another effect of the size is to preclude fin stabilisation: the total size of the plastic explosive, added to the long tail and the large fins required to stabilise it, will probably be too great ever to result in a practical fin stabilised round. It would appear that it is confined to being spin stabilised from a rifled barrel. This makes it the odd man out in anti-armour projectiles because HEAT warheads are better fin stabilised.

HEAT Projectiles

HEAT projectiles are in wide use in anti-tank weapons. The outstanding advantage of this design is that deep penetration is possible from a comparatively small amount of explosive and consequently a light weight projectile. Their use extends from 125 mm tank guns to shoulder launched anti-tank rockets weighing less than 3 kgs. The basic components of the HEAT warhead, perhaps more descriptively called a hollow charge warhead, are illustrated in Fig. 10.

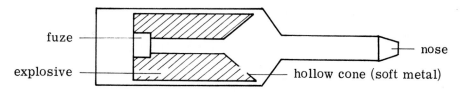

Fig. 10 Components of a HEAT projectile

The object of this design is to produce a narrow jet of gases, containing metal particles, which blasts its way through the armour and splays bits of armour, referred to as spall, from the inside of the armour.

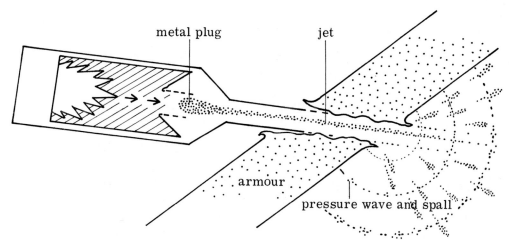

Fig. 11 HEAT effect

To allow the jet to form properly the warhead must be properly detonated at an optimum stand-off distance. This is achieved by placing the fuze actuator on a probe. When it contacts the armour, a fuze at the centre of the cone base initiates the explosive. The cone shape concentrates the resulting gases into a jet which contains some particles from the cone metal, which is often made of copper. The remainder of the cone forms a plug which follows the jet. Performance can be varied by changes in the cone material, the cone angle and the cone diameter. Using a rule of thumb guide, penetration is approximately three or four times the diameter of the cone, though modern devices can probably exceed this.

HEAT projectiles are better fin stabilised than spin stabilised because a rotating
jet would spread out and be less effective. It is thus better fired from a smooth
bore gun, but, using the same slipping driving band device as on the APFSDS, the
HEAT projectile can also be fired from a rifled barrel. HEAT warheads are used
in most anti-tank guided weapons (ATGW) and shoulder launched anti-tank rockets;
also they are commonly used in sub-munitions and mines, as is their cousin the
plate charge.

Plate Charges

The plate charge can also be referred to as the 'P' charge, a Self Forging
Fragment or the Miznay Schardin effect. It relies on blowing a dished plate, at a
very high velocity, against the armour and punching a hole through it. Although
its penetration is much less than that of a HEAT warhead, if it penetrates it
creates more damage behind the armour with the combined effect of the plate itself and the bits of armour it has knocked out. A diagrammatic explanation of its
operation is in Fig. 12.

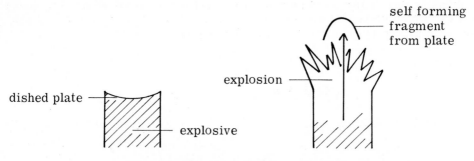

Fig. 12 Miznay Schardin operation

It is being used more and more in mines and sub-munitions in which it is of particular use because it is effective even when detonated some distance from the
target.

Carrier Projectiles

The time-proved contents of carrier projectiles are smokes of many colours,
illumination, incendiary, flare cannister and propaganda. More recently nuclear
chemical, biological, radar echo and sub-munitions have been added to the invent-
ory. It is worth mentioning three types: smokes, illuminants and chemicals.
Sub-munitions will be dealt with separately.

To obtain an instant smoke screen a bursting smoke projectile is best. Its main
constituent is normally white phosphorous or sometimes red phosphorous (RP)
which also has unpleasant anti-personnel burning effects. It has the disadvantages
of dissipating quickly and pillaring into the air rather than keeping to the ground.
Slower developing smokes produce a more lasting smoke screen; their main
constituent is normally hexachlorethene. Coloured smokes are used for target

indication and signalling.   Typical WP exploding and base ejection (BE) projectile layouts are given in Fig. 13.

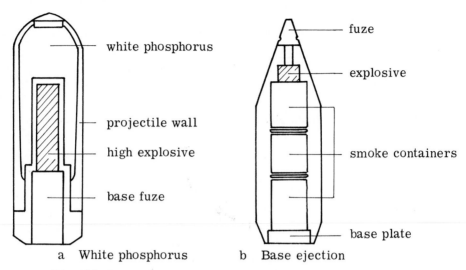

white phosphorus

projectile wall

high explosive

base fuze

fuze

explosive

smoke containers

base plate

a   White phosphorus   b   Base ejection

Fig. 13 Examples of WP and BE smoke projectiles

Chemical fillings are produced by both the USSR and the United States.   They are normally of a similar construction to that carrying WP.

The most common projectiles throw out a parachute suspending a cannister.   The contents are normally magnesium, which burns for a very long time: its light intensity is dependent on its size.   Illumination projectiles come in a wide variety of forms and sizes from hand launched rockets, through small and large mortar bombs, to shells of all sizes.   Coloured illuminants can be produced by using salts of barium to provide green, strontium for red and sodium for yellow.

Sub-munitions

Increasingly, ammunition designers are turning to the use of bomblets, grenade-lets and minelets conveyed in a carrier shell, bomb or rocket.   In general terms, because of the reduced stresses, it is easier to design bombs or rocket and SSGW warheads to carry sub-munitions than it is to design shells, but all have been achieved.   Fig. 14 shows the outline configuration of the US 155 mm M483 shell. When the ejection charge explodes the bomblets are ejected through the base over the target.   In Fig. 15 a typical bomblet, which in this case has a primary anti-armour and secondary anti-personnel role, is illustrated, but the same principle of design applies to all carrier warheads, no matter what their contents may be.

The advantages gained from sub-munitions are a better spread on the ground of fragments from grenadelets or, because of their number, a better chance of hit by bomblets or minelets.   The last two, also, attack weak roof and belly parts of armoured vehicles.   Many sub-munitions, under a variety of labels and

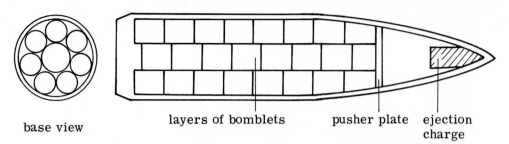

base view   layers of bomblets   pusher plate   ejection charge

Fig. 14 American 155 mm M483 shell. Basic configuration

abbreviations, are being developed and when their hit chance is improved in the future, through the use of micro-electronic seeker and guidance systems, they may well play a deciding part in mechanised battles.

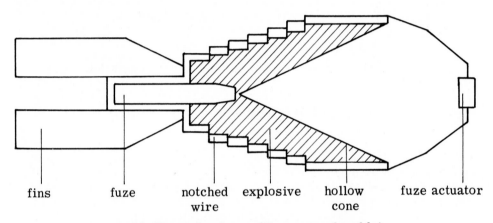

fins   fuze   notched explosive   hollow   fuze actuator

                      wire   cone

Fig. 15 Example of a multi-purpose bomblet

FUZES AND EXPLOSIVE TRAINS FOR PROJECTILES

So far we have looked at the warheads but not at the way they are detonated. The same principles apply to the initiation of a warhead as to the propellant which was described earlier in this chapter. Again the train goes from a sensitive explosive through intermediaries which become less sensitive until the main charge or filling is detonated or released. The difference is that a warhead has a fuze, which carries out special functions of which a soldier is most concerned about two: these are reliability and safety. Reliability is essential if troops are to trust their artillery's effectiveness, which may be critical to success in the attack and survival in defence. Obtaining reliability, despite the difficult conditions in which ammunition may be stored and transported on the battlefield, demands very careful design and manufacture, otherwise the warhead will not go off when required. It would be even more disastrous and demoralising if it went off when it was not required to do so! Safety is the most important characteristic of any fuze.

To ensure extreme safety, fuzes normally have two stages of safety incorporated
in them. In the simplest warheads the first stage may be a safety pin, similar to
that in a grenade, which can be withdrawn by hand. In projectiles fired from guns,
the first stage is normally released by the setback action on firing or the centrifugal effect of the projectile's spin. A device which illustrates both is shown in
Fig. 16.

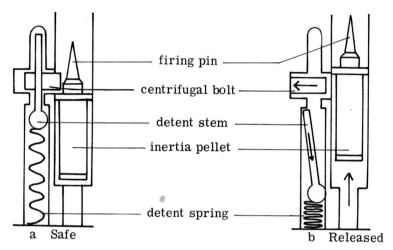

firing pin

centrifugal bolt

detent stem

inertia pellet

detent spring

a   Safe   b   Released

Fig. 16   Example of a fuze safety device

As the projectile is accelerated up the barrel and away, the detent is set back
against its retaining spring and it slips out of a centrifugal bolt. In its turn the
bolt is moved outwards along its horizontal channel by centrifugal force as the
projectile spins. The firing pin is then free for the next stage.

The next stage of safety is final and its removal results in detonation. In Fig. 16,
which shows a graze fuze, there is a heavy firing pin. It is hurled forward on to
the detonator when the warhead grazes or hits the ground and is decelerated. In
simpler fuzes, when the warhead strikes the target or the ground, the striker is
forced back on to a detonator. Systems in which an electrical circuit is completed, when the projectile impacts, are also used.

Becoming more common are air burst warheads because they are much more
effective than ground burst. There are two main types of fuze which are used
for air bursts. The first is a proximity fuze, which employs a small radar: it
puts out a signal which measures the distance from the ground and, at a preset
distance, it triggers. A similar effect can be achieved by a time fuze, which is
set before firing to measure the time of flight from the gun. It can be mechanical
similar to a clock or work on the time taken to burn through a safety fuze. If all
the gun data calculations are correct, the projectile will then detonate at the
correct height.

The technology of fuzes has now become quite extensive and this chapter gives
only a bare outline, but Volume 3 of the series deals with the subject in more
detail.

MINES

A section on mines is included in this chapter to complete the review of ammunition. A whole chapter is given over to the subject in Volume 3, but this section will be confined to a quick look at the characteristics of anti-tank and anti-personnel mines.

Anti-tank Mines

The three ways of attacking a tank or any vehicle with a mine are by cutting the tracks or blowing off the wheels, going for the belly, or going for the side.

To attack the track of a tank, a mine requires approximately 3 kg of explosive at least, but normally they have two or three times that amount. In its simplest form it is initiated by a pressure fuze. Surprisingly, a belly attack mine needs much less explosive when it employs the shaped charge or Miznay Schardin effect. Miznay Schardin mines can be effective with 1 kg of explosive. However, a belly attack mine needs a more complicated fuze than one designed only to cut tracks. It can be set off by vertical rods which are broken or bent by the tank hull or by small wires or hoses spread about horizontally on the ground and set off when two of them are pressured by tank tracks. Neither of these are easily concealed but this can be achieved if the more advanced influence fuzes are used, operating on the heat, sound, seismic or magnetic effects of the tank to set them off.

Similar complicated fuzes can be used to actuate the off-route mine which attacks the side of a tank, but it can be actuated by a simple trip wire. The wire itself can be attached to an anti-tank rocket, a hollow charge device or a Miznay Schardin device.

The whole business of anti-tank mining and countering becomes a matter of outwitting the opposing designer. Rollers and flails carried by tanks are countered by double impulse fuzes; ploughs, as frequently used on Russian tanks, are countered by tilt and anti-disturbance fuzes. Plastic bodied mines, like the British barmine, are used to defeat metal detectors. Anti-tank mining, and its countermeasures, is a military expertise of its own. The use of anti-personnel mines in conjunction with them is yet another complication.

Anti-personnel Mines

Anti-personnel mines can be designed to blow off a foot or leg when stepped upon. They can also be made to jump up and spray pellets or chopped wire at body height when actuated by trip wire or, as in the case of a Claymore mine, be placed against some vertical feature, such as a tree or fence, and spray out small steel balls when command detonated. The smallest, which damage a foot, can contain as little as 8 grams of explosive while the largest, such as the Claymore, may contain up to nearly 700 grams.

Laying Minefields

Up to the 1939 - 45 war, minefields were laid by hand and normally the mines were buried to complicate detection. With the advent of highly mobile warfare, faster laying methods are used and concealment is often sacrificed to the need for speed. Anti-tank mines are commonly laid from vehicles by means of a mechanical layer. Fig. 17 shows a British Barmine Layer in action behind the FV 432 APC. The United States has now gone one stage further by developing a capability to scatter mines from helicopters and shells which can carry Remotely Delivered Mines (RDM).

Fig. 17 Barmine Layer being pulled by FV 432 APC

Ranger, pictured in Fig. 18, is a British method of laying anti-personnel mines at a considerable speed by projecting them from launchers on top of the FV 432 APC. Such an APC can pull the barmine layer as well and so produce, rapidly, a mixed minefield.

Fig. 18 Ranger on FV 432 APC

CONCLUSION

This chapter has reviewed the field of ammunition. Information in it is relevant to the chapters covering Small Arms, Artillery Systems, Guided Weapons, Vehicles and NBC.

SELF TEST QUESTIONS

Question 1   What are the main categories of complete rounds of ammunition?

                  Answer ....

                         ....

                         ....

Question 2   What are the main components of a typical explosive train in a cartridge?

                  Answer ....

                         ....

                         ....

Question 3   What are the main arguments for adopting a smooth bore gun?

                  Answer ....

                         ....

                         ....

Question 4   Why has a fin stabilised HESH round not been produced to date?

                  Answer ....

                         ....

                         ....

                         ....

Question 5   What relationship is there between the diameter of a hollow charge warhead and the thickness of armour it can penetrate?

                  Answer ....

                         ....

                         ....

Question 6   In what type of munitions is the Miznay Schardin effect most used?

Answer ....

....

Question 7   What type of munitions are to be found in carrier projectiles?

Answer ....

....

....

....

....

....

....

....

Question 8   What are the two main requirements of a fuze?

Answer ....

....

Question 9   What are the main methods by which mines damage armoured
vehicles?

Answer ....

....

....

Question 10   What methods are now available for producing minefields?

Answer ....

....

....

....

....

ANSWERS ON PAGE 178

4

Nuclear, Biological and Chemical Warfare

INTRODUCTION

If some governments consider that war is too important to be left to generals then all governments must consider that nuclear, chemical or biological warfare must be controlled by the highest level of government. This has happened and it can be seen that whereas the threat of war was a negotiator's tool in the past, now it appears there are several tools in the bag, increasing in clout from the use of conventional warfare, through the use of chemical warfare and tactical nuclear warfare to strategic nuclear warfare. To complicate the situation Strategic Arms Limitation Talks (SALT) now, despite the title, must include discussion of theatre nuclear weapons like the SS 20 and cruise missiles as well as the strategic weapons.

So far only USSR, the United States, Britain, France, China and India have demonstrated their possession of nuclear weapons, but many more, including Australia, Canada, Italy, South Africa, Israel and Pakistan have the technological capability to produce them. Only the United States and the USSR admit to producing chemical weapons, but they are relatively easy and cheap to produce and within the capability of most arms producing countries to do so. A veil of silence seems to be drawn over biological weapons' capabilities, but we will consider them briefly after we have looked at nuclear and chemical weapons. Each type of weapon is best dealt with separately because they are quite different in all ways except as negotiators' tools.

NUCLEAR WEAPONS

The whole spectrum of effects produced by a nuclear weapon is wide and varied. The scale of them is vast and, in the view of many, utterly disastrous. This gives rise to a variety of approaches by nations to the problem of protecting their civilian population from the effect of a nuclear attack. Some take the fatalistic view that the effects would be so catastrophic that nothing could be done; others like Sweden and Switzerland take extensive measures. If, however, military forces are to remain credible in the face of the threat imposed by nuclear weapons, they must first have a capability to reply themselves, thus deterring their opponents, and second they must understand the effects of the nuclear weapons, how to sur-vive attack by them and how to fight on after their use. Warsaw Pact and NATO forces both possess the deterrent and both train to survive in a nuclear environ-ment. This is what the remainder of this section will survey.

Nuclear Weapons Effects

The effects in which a soldier is interested are those which affect himself and his equipment. Both would be affected by the immediate blast heat and radiation which a nuclear weapon would create; the soldier would then be concerned about the effect of residual radiation on himself and that of the immediate Electro-Magnetic Pulse (EMP) and the Transient Radiation Effects on Electronics (TREE) on his electronic equipment.

All effects are very dependent upon the height of the burst above Ground Zero (GZ) which is the point on the ground at which the burst takes place or immediately under the burst. A ground burst describes one in which the fireball touches the ground; all others are air bursts. We will consider the effects of blast, heat and radiation in turn.

Blast Effects

Approximately 50% of the energy given out by a nuclear explosion appears as blast; it is similar to that produced by a conventional explosion, except for its scale. The terms used to describe nuclear effects often hide their enormity: a kiloton (KT) warhead is a very small nuclear device indeed, but it is the equiv-alent of one thousand tons of TNT explosive. The nuclear bomb dropped at Nagasaki was about 22 KT, which in strategic weapon terms of megatons is still small, but it may best be imagined again in terms of TNT: it would take a convoy of 2,200 medium sized lorries, each carrying 10 tons, to carry the explosive required!

The blast wave from a nuclear burst travels outwards like the shell of a sphere. When it hits the ground it is reflected: the reflected wave combines with the orig-inal blast wave and so the final wave travelling along the ground is in fact quite complicated, composed of atmospheric overpressures and wind: a more detailed description of it is given in Volume 4 of the series. Apart from the size of the device, the height of burst is obviously the next most important factor in deter-mining the force of that blast wave. Graphs can be constructed relating an opti-mum height of burst to the yield of the device and the effect caused at particular distances: planners use such graphs.

As the blast wave goes over a target there are several effects on that target. Perhaps the easiest way to imagine it is to consider a group of soldiers resting in a barn. The overpressure would tend to crush the barn and the wind would tend to push it over or even blow it away completely. As the atmosphere around the explosion recovered, the air would be sucked back towards the centre and there would be a smaller effect caused by a sudden drop in atmosphere pressure and a wind blowing towards the explosion for a short time. Although these second

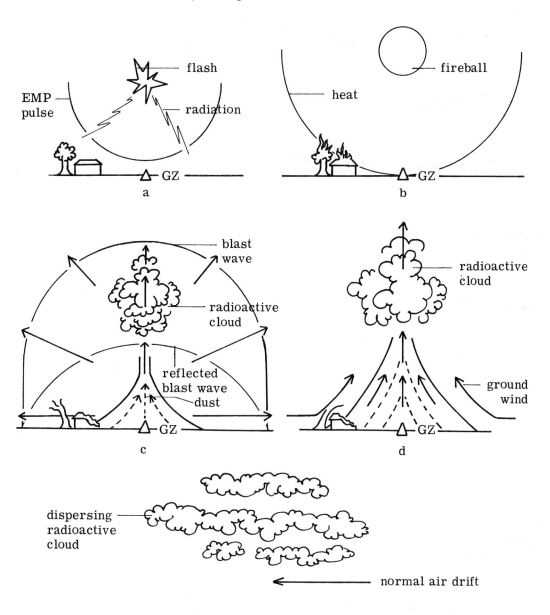

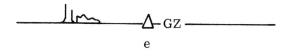

Fig. 1 Development of a nuclear airburst

effects would be noticeable they would not be of sufficient significance to cause damage to military targets.

The primary effects of blast on man is remarkably little. Approximately half of soldiers' eardrums would burst when the pressure of the air reached between 7 and 15 lbs per sq in (psi) above normal atmospheric pressure (over-pressure): it is not expected that this would make a man immediately unbattleworthy. The next level at which the soldier would be harmed is at approximately 40 psi over-pressure when damage to lungs and other parts of the body would occur. The wind effect on him is not to be dismissed when it is realized that the wind could reach speeds of two or three times those which prevail at the height of a hurricane. Parts of the body might snap when the blast wave hits a man, but the secondary effects such as being hurled into something stationary, being hit by flying debris or being rattled about in a vehicle which was turned over would probably cause more casualties. In Fig. 2 the table shows the approximate distance for a 1 KT and a 1 MT device at which 50% of the men and their equipments would be sufficiently damaged to become unbattleworthy or require repair in a workshop before they would be battleworthy again.

Type of equipment	1 KT Device			1 MT Device		
	Optimum height of burst	Range	Over pressure	Optimum height of burst	Range	Over pressure
Soft vehicles	170 m	300 m	18 psi	1900 m	4800 m	9 psi
Artillery in the open	170 m	200 m	30 psi	1900 m	3200 m	17.5 psi
Tanks	150 m	170 m	45 psi	1800 m	2700 m	22 psi
Men in open	200 m	355 m	15 psi	2000 m	5700 m	7 psi

Fig. 2 Blast effects: range at which 50% of men will become unbattleworthy or their equipments will require workshop repairs.

As expected the range at which the level of damage occurs is considerably more for a MT device but not 1,000 times greater. It is, in fact, only approximately 10 - 15 times greater and from this we can deduce that there is a law of diminishing returns. Yet another phenomenon which can be seen in the Fig. 2 table is that the over-pressure which causes the damage in the case of a 1 MT device is considerably less than for a 1 KT. The reason is the blast wave is longer, takes longer to pass over a target and so affects it for a greater time.

There is one effect from blast which we have not yet considered: that is the shock wave which would travel through the ground, much like an earthquake effect, if the burst were on or near the ground. The resultant ground shockwave would travel much faster than the blast wave in the air but its destructive range would be less; how much less would depend upon the type of ground. Foundations, trenches and underground structures such as cellars and sewers would be damaged and all the normal damage associated with earthquakes would occur.

Primary and secondary effects of blast would account for approximately 35% of the total casualties from a 20 KT airburst. About another 50% could be caused by the thermal effects: heat and light.

Thermal Effects

Few people have not seen a film of a nuclear explosion which begins with a bright flash and a ball of fire which rapidly climbs, sucking up dust from the ground after it to form the typical nuclear mushroom cloud. No matter how well the film is taken and processed, it cannot portray the intense brightness of the flash or the fearsome heat which the fireball emits. The flash is many times brighter than the midday sun and the temperature of the fireball is over $1,000,000^{\circ}C$

Fig. 3 A nuclear explosion

The effects of the flash differ greatly depending on whether it is day or night, whether the visibility is affected by mist and rain, and the duration of the flash which is dependent on the power of the explosion, the distance from the ground zero and the general topography. In very rough general terms a man facing the flash in daylight would probably suffer from temporary blindness for approximately two minutes: at night it would be approximately ten minutes before his sight recovered. Approximately 1 in 1,000 would suffer a form of permanent blindness in one or both eyes, but in military terms this is not the main problem, the main concern is with such men as drivers and pilots who could be in great danger until their sight returns. Research is directed at a quick acting shutter and goggles which turn opaque or darken like certain types of sun-glasses: but as the flash travels at the speed of light the problem is hard to solve.

The effect of heat on men and equipment is very difficult to predict. First of all it depends upon the yield of warhead which determines the size of the fireball. A 1 KT yield would produce a fireball with a diameter of 140 m whilst a 1 MT yield would result in one with a 2,200 m diameter. Obviously any target which was engulfed by the fireball itself would be totally destroyed. Beyond the fireball the thermal effects can be divided into flash effects and flame effects. The flash is thermal energy containing x-rays, ultra-violet rays, light-rays and infra-red (IR) rays. It travels at the speed of light (300,000 km/s or 186,000 miles/s). At 820 m from a 1 KT burst the exposed skin of a man would suffer second degree burns: this means that it would be blistered to a certain extent and destroyed to a certain extent, taking up to three weeks treatment to heal. The same effect would be caused by a 1 MT weapon at 19,000 m from the burst. However, even the leaf of a tree or a sheet of paper could provide protection from the flash if it were between the burst and the man's skin. Clothing would protect it completely. Obviously, therefore, the best way for a clothed man to protect himself would be to turn away or, better still, to lie down with his hands underneath him.

The ranges quoted would be considerably reduced if weather conditions, such as rain or fog, were involved. Men in vehicles or buildings would be completely pro-tected from flash effects unless they were in the direct line of an opening like a vehicle hatch or a window. Again the topography would have a great bearing on the effects: flat country would not provide so much protection as rolling or hilly country; nor would open country provide so much as wooded or built-up areas. It means that it is hard for an aggressor or a defender to forecast the effects of flash with any certainty.

The same difficulty applies equally to flame effects which are the burnings result-ing from equipment or buildings set on fire by the flash. Dry grass or other growth is relatively easily set alight; cotton or wool clothing is harder to ignite, but not so difficult as vehicle canopies. Burning clothing can normally be extin-guished easily but vehicle canopies and other materials which surround a soldier are not so easily stopped. Just to confuse the situation more, fires could some-times be blown out by the blast wave which, travelling more slowly, arrives after the thermal flash and consequential fires.

So far it can be seen that outside the main catastrophic area of destruction caused by a nuclear device the effects of thermal radiation and blast are hard to fore-cast. Let us now consider radiation effects.

Radiation and its Effects

Although radiation raises the most emotive discussion of any of the nuclear effects, it is not necessarily the most lethal. Indeed, taking a 20 KT airburst, an average of only approximately 15% of casualties would be caused by it. This figure would vary with the height of burst and size of yield, but first it is worth considering the various types of radiation which are grouped under the two main headings 'immediate radiation' and 'residual radiation'. 'Immediate radiation' is that which has an effect within 60 seconds of the burst.

Under immediate radiation come alpha particles, beta particles, gamma radiation and neutron radiation. The start point of all is the atom and a quick study of it will help.

When the atom "breaks" the various bits of debris form the radiation. The first type, alpha particles, each consist of two protons and two neutrons from the nucleus of the atom (see Fig. 4). These can be stopped by any obstruction, even a sheet of paper, and are thus of no military significance. The second type, beta particles, are electrons: they have a little more penetration than alpha particles and can cause damage, in the form of a sort of burn, to the skin. They are not, in military terms, lethal and their effects are not immediate because they only travel a few metres through air. As we shall see later, they can, on the other hand, be incapacitating. For now we are left with neutron and gamma radiation.

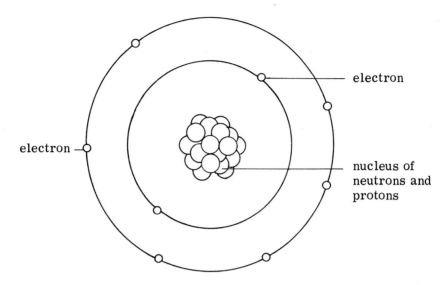

Fig. 4 Basic constituents of an atom

Neutron radiation is, as the name implies, a stream of neutrons from the nucleus of an atom and gamma radiation is composed of electromagnetic waves, similar to radio waves and X-rays but of shorter wavelength. Neutron and gamma radiation are the radiation casualty inflictors and may travel several thousand metres through air.

Radiation is measured in rads. It is estimated that no acute effects would be caused by a radiation dose of under 200 rads. A dose of 200 - 500 rads would cause incapacitation after approximately one week and many of the casualties would die. A higher dose of 500 - 1,000 rads would cause incapacitation within four days and most of the casualties would die.

It should be mentioned that doses of radiation are, on the whole, cumulative. This means that a soldier who received a nuclear dose of 250 rads on one day, followed by a 300 rad dose on a succeeding day would most probably die. It appears, however, that the body can slowly recover after a sub-lethal dose, but the recovery time is measured in weeks rather than days.

Protection from Immediate Radiation

Some protection from immediate radiation can be effected by any form of shield between the nuclear burst and the victim. The more material and the denser the material the better: lead would provide a most efficient shield; water, steel and most of all earth, would all be good protection. In very general terms a soft vehicle does not provide much protection against gamma radiation. However, a tank gives four times as much protection, an open trench five times as much and a trench with normal overhead cover fifty times as much. For the first time we must introduce the idea that there may be different effects on men caused by neutron and gamma radiation. This is because neutron radiation, as it is stopped by shielding, produces some gamma radiation which carries on. Thus, for example, the shield provided by a tank's armour against the neutron radiation is only three times as effective (and not four, as against gamma) as that provided by a soft vehicle. It can now be seen that a device which could be designed to produce more neutron radiation at the expense of other nuclear effects could well be very effective against armoured formations. This is the concept behind the much publicised neutron bomb, and the reason why the Russians, with their preponderance of armoured vehicles, reacted so strongly against its introduction onto the battlefield.

Under average visibility conditions the radiation from a 1 KT airburst would be approximately as shown in Fig. 5.

	500 m	1,000 m	2,000 m	4,000 m
1 KT	5,000 rads	200 rads	1.5 rads	.03 rads
10 KT	50,000 rads	2,000 rads	15 rads	.3 rads
100 KT	750,000 rads	300,000 rads	22,500 rads	4.5 rads

Fig. 5 Radiation doses at various ranges

It can be seen from this table that a soldier will not suffer potentially lethal effects, (ie more than 200 rads) from a 1 KT burst at more than 1 km from it. Approximately 15% of casualties from a 20 KT airburst would be caused by radiation, both immediate and residual.

Residual Radiation

Residual radiation is found on the ground beneath a ground burst and in fallout from the dust cloud spreading out from the nuclear mushroom cloud. That on the ground is mainly gamma and beta radiation. Its military significance is the denial of ground it would cause or even a denial of transit. The rate at which radiation reduces or decays is indicated below.

H + 1 hr	2,000 rads/hr
H + 7 hr	200 rads/hr
H + 2 days	20 rads/hr
H + 2 weeks	2 rads/hr

Monitoring of the radiation would normally take place before entering into an irradiated area.

Residual radiation in fallout is in fact radioactive particles from the warhead. The resultant cloud of radioactivity is at the mercy of the vagaries of the weather. Rain or snow will bring the radiation to the ground comparatively quickly, but a wind may blow it some distance before it comes to the earth. This type of radiation is gamma and beta by nature and the cause of casualties will be skin burns and from swallowing food or drink which has had radioactive fallout on it.

Residual radiation is only militarily significant if the fireball has touched the ground, when it becomes a groundburst. An airburst produces insignificant radiation on the ground around its GZ. Nor does it produce any significant fallout because the fireball rises rapidly; consequently the vapourised radioactive elements of the warhead condense into microparticles which are dispersed into the higher atmosphere and fall to the ground slowly. Their radioactivity decays, they are dispersed by the winds, fall world-wide and are scarcely detectable.

Assuming, however, that a ground burst occurs, then methods must be designed to predict the hazard to troops crossing the radioactive area around the GZ and from fallout. This is dealt with fully in Volume 4 of the series. For now we can see that predictions of residual radiation around the GZ can be made if the height of the burst and the yield is known. Fallout can also be predicted to a certain extent if wind directions and strengths are known. It is not an exact science and where possible trained reconnaissance troops with monitoring equipment would confirm predictions.

Overall Effects of Nuclear Explosions Against Men

As we have seen, the lethality of all three effects, blast, thermal and radiation vary considerably depending upon the yield, height of burst, weather conditions, the topography, the type of protection or shield available and standard of training of the troops. To produce an impression of the relative lethality of the three effects, Fig. 6 gives the radii around GZ at which unwarned and unprotected men in combat dress would be rendered ineffective for combat by a 1 KT, a 15 KT and a 150 KT airburst.

It is apparent that in the case of a relatively small explosion of 1 KT, the range of radiation effects is most prominent; a 15 KT explosion's effects are beginning to be dominated by thermal and at 150 KT the range of thermal effects is nearly twice that of blast and three times that of radiation.

Fig. 7 shows a similar distribution for tanks and men in them. In this case the radiation effects are dominant until the 150 KT size is reached. Then the huge blast effect is able to damage tanks and consequently the men in them at a range of 1,225 m. Unless the tanks are touched by the fireball, the thermal effects will be swamped by the blast and radiation. However, the ability of radiation to affect armoured forces again indicates why a neutron bomb, in which the design of the device is optimised to produce radiation at the expense of blast and thermal effects, could be a very effective weapon against Warsaw Pact armies.

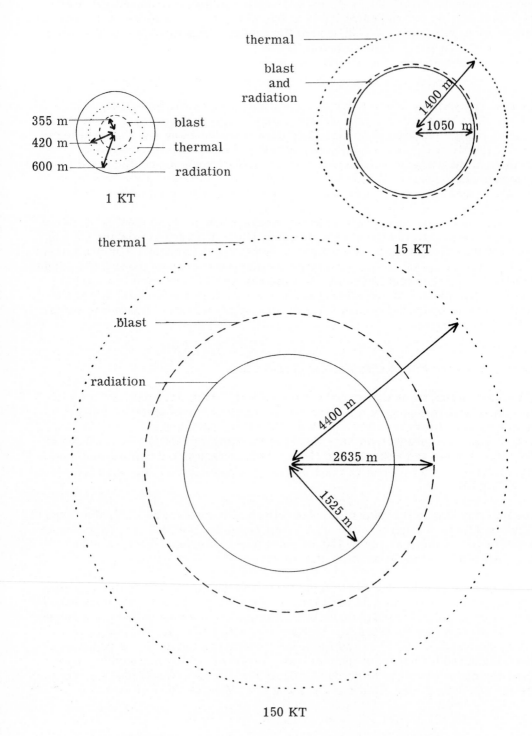

Fig. 6 Airburst nuclear effects ranges against unprotected men

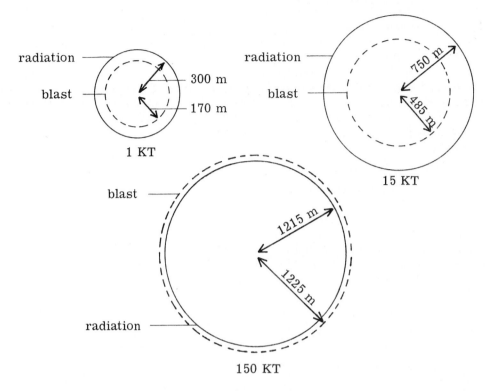

Fig. 7 Airburst nuclear effects ranges against tanks and the men in them

Electromagnetic Effects on Equipment

There are two main electromagnetic effects of a nuclear explosion. The first is the electromagnetic pulse (EMP) which can damage electronic equipment and the second is the change it can make to the electrical conductivity of the atmosphere and ionosphere.

If a nuclear device were exploded at a height of more than 100 km the EMP would cover a huge area, of continental size, and could cause severe disruption in communications and electronic equipment. A change in electrical conductivity of the ionosphere and atmosphere would affect high frequency (HF) communications very considerably to the extent that they might be unworkable. Low (LF) and medium (MF) frequency communications would also be down-graded. Very high frequency (VHF) and ultra high frequency (UHF) communications would not be adversely affected. On the other hand radar effectiveness would deteriorate.

The other effect of electromagnetic radiation is on the electronic components of such equipments as radios, radars and computers. This goes under the generic term of Transient Radiation Effects on Electronic Equipments (TREE). It manifests itself by corrupting computer magnetic stores, tripping relays, causing insulation failures in cable and burnouts in signal equipment.

Protection Against Nuclear Effects

If troops are in the open then the only effective defence against blast, thermal or radiation is, on sensing the flash, for them to throw themselves flat facing downwards away from the burst with their hands under them. When they are not in the open, and a nuclear attack is possible, then troops should rest in cellars, trenches with overhead cover or heavily armoured vehicles with closed hatches. A considerable amount can be achieved to protect electronic equipment if thought is given to prevent TREE (this process is called nuclear hardening). Shielding, short leads, avoidance of loops and the provision of electronic filters can all be designed into new equipment to mitigate TREE.

CHEMICAL WARFARE

Chemical warfare was first used in the 1914 - 18 war and had a demoralising effect, not only on the units who suffered casualties, but also on those troops who saw the gas sufferers being evacuated. The effect on morale is one of the great factors which must be considered when training to deal with chemical warfare (CW) and good training is one of the best ways to ensure that morale will be sustained in the face of a chemical attack.

Fig. 8 British soldiers in NBC protective clothing

A form of truce held in the 1939 - 45 war, either by a desire to stand by the Geneva gas protocol of 1925 or because a form of deterrent existed: both sides possessed the capability to field chemical weapons. Indeed the great problem of chemical weapons is that the chemicals themselves can be produced by any nation able to produce insecticides, which resemble them, and then they can be put in weapons by nations capable of producing a white phosphorus (WP) shell: Chapter 3 gives the outline design of such a shell.

The effectiveness of a chemical attack can be reduced by good personal and collective protective equipment. Warsaw Pact countries and those of NATO have developed such equipment, with Great Britain in the forefront of it. The problem is that troop formations who are dressed and closed down in a protective posture lose much of their combat effectiveness. It can be seen that the men dressed in full protective equipment as shown in Fig. 8 are not nearly so agile nor able to use their weapons and equipment with the ease of an unprotected man.

If one protagonist in a war possessed an offensive capability whilst his opponent possessed only a defensive capability then the nation with the offensive capability would have a considerable advantage. At present, between Warsaw Pact and NATO countries, a deterrent exists because the USSR and the United States both possess an offensive capability. Whether or not other nations should develop an offensive capability is a matter for discussion.

Tactical Uses of Chemical Agents

As with nuclear weapons, chemical agents can be used as an immediate offensive weapon or as a method of denying a piece of ground to an enemy by contaminating it. As indicated above it can also be used to reduce the combat effectiveness of a foe by forcing him to close down and don full protective clothing. The chemical agents can be delivered much as HE or smoke in mortar bombs, shells, rockets and bombs. To create the necessary tactical effects there are a variety of agents causing different effects. To deny ground a persistent agent, slow to disperse, is required. For an immediate offensive effect, followed by an attack, a non-persistent agent which will evaporate quickly is necessary.

The Nature of Chemical Agents

There is a wide variety of ways in which chemical agents attack the human physiology. Phosgene is a choking agent which attacks the respiratory tract and lungs; hydrogen cyanide interferes with the blood's ability to carry oxygen; adamsite causes violent vomiting; mustard gas causes very painful blisters; nerve agents cause muscular spasms and paralysis; finally CS and CR cause irritation of the eyes and respiratory tracts. The last two of these are merely incapacitating agents and of more use in riot control than full scale war. Mustard gas on the other hand, although not lethal is a damaging agent and persistent. Its effect is to deny the use of ground or even the use of contaminated material. The nerve agents, which are chemically based on phosphorus, vary in their tactical application: all are lethal and rapid acting; Tabun (GA) is fairly persistent whilst VX definitely is persistent and can be absorbed through the skin; Sarin (GB) and Soman (GD) are more persistent.

They are all so unpleasant and incapacitating that perhaps the only important consideration for the soldier, apart from the tactical employment, is the speed of their effect: nerve gases are the quickest to put a soldier out of action.

Storage Problems

Although not at first sight a serious military problem, the storage of lethal chemical weapons is important because many governments are concerned about the danger of storing chemical weapons on their territory and later the difficulty of disposing of them when they become outdated. To overcome these concerns the development of binary chemical weapons is being studied. The concept is that the final, lethal agent is composed of two chemicals, each of which is harm-less by itself. The two chemicals are kept apart, perhaps within a warhead and only made to mix, to produce the lethal agent, when in flight towards the target.

Protection

To ensure his personal protection a soldier requires to cover all his skin and his clothing with a NBC suit, overshoes and gloves in addition to wearing a respirator. This, as we have mentioned before, reduces a soldier's combat ability and it is not feasible that he can wear his respirator all the time. His best defence, there-fore, is for him to assume that any shelling, mortaring or bombing attack is a chemical attack until tests can be made to prove otherwise. Such a policy entails the donning of respirators until tests are made with detector papers, which are dye impregnated papers which change colour when affected by CW agents, or with Residual Vapour Detectors (RVD). The RVD works by drawing air through an indicator pad which reacts by changing colour: different CW agents give different colour reactions. When there is no reaction, off come the respirators.

British and Soviet AFVs are normally fitted with NBC packs which give collective protection to the crews. They operate by drawing all the air through a filter which removes CW agents. The crew compartments are slightly pressurised to prevent any contaminated air creeping in through weapon apertures or hatches. Obviously, collective protection makes living for long periods in a chemically contaminated environment a far more reasonable proposition than when dressed up in a NBC suit and respirator. On the other hand the equipments to provide the collective protection are costly, bulky and use scarce vehicle power supplies. Certainly once vehicles' protections are broken by the entry of contaminated men or ammunition, then the crews must revert to personal protection and don their NBC suits and respirators. The United States is not so convinced as Britain that collective protection is essential.

An alarm system for chemical agents has been developed in the United States and in the United Kingdom where it is called the Nerve Agent Immobilised Enzyme Alarm and Detector (NAIAD). If used upwind, such devices can give sufficient warning of attack to allow protective measures to be taken.

So far we have not mentioned any medical methods which prevent the agents work-ing (prophylaxis) or cure a casualty (therapy). Oximes can act as a prophylactic against nerve agents. Because they are rapidly excreted they must be taken regularly to keep a prophylactic level in the body. Atropine, injected immediately the effects of a nerve agent are recognised, can be an effective therapy: British soldiers are issued with atropine syringes.

Conclusion

The USSR has ammunition stocks of CW agents held well forward ready for use. It is known that they have 1914 - 18 agents such as hydrogen cyanide and mustard gas; they also have more modern nerve agents, which they learned about when they overran the German plant on the Polish frontier in 1945: they transported that plant, complete with its staff, to Russia.

Providing a deterrent, the United States forces possess a wide armoury of CW ammunition of most types. Both the Warsaw Pact and the NATO armies have developed protective equipment and practise its use. On the other hand only the USSR is known to possess a biological warfare (BW) capability: the United States has foresworn its use.

BIOLOGICAL WARFARE

Biological Agents and their Effectiveness

Biological warfare (BW) can be said to have been used ever since one tribe poisoned its enemy's water supply or provided it with poisoned food. In modern times it is known that the Warsaw Pact trains in the use of biological warfare and trains in civil defence against it.

Biological warfare today is the creation of diseases like Dengue Fever by virus, Epidemic Typhus by rickettsiae, Cholera by bacteria or Coccidioidomycosis by fungus. The problem for the instigator of biological warfare is that the diseases take from 2 - 21 days to take effect and so it is not suitable for effective tactical weapons: chemical warfare would be much more efficient. It is possible, however, to imagine that BW could be used strategically to cripple a population at a critical moment of preparation for war.

Dissemination of Biological Agents

Biological agents could be spread covertly or overtly by spray tanks which released the agents into the slipstream of an aircraft. A compressor which forced agents out into an aerosol cloud from a nozzle could be operated from a ship. It is also possible for agents to be delivered in shells or bombs. Although most of the organisms would be killed by the explosion of such devices, even if only 1% survived, there would be sufficient to spread a great deal of disease. Any of these delivery methods could be used strategically.

Protection

It would be possible, in theory, to sample large volumes of air to test for biological agents, but this would take so long that casualties would occur before a warning could be given and prophylactic action taken. Even if it were, immunisation
or the use of antibiotics would not be possible in time because the wide range of
vaccines required and the limited effectiveness of antibiotics against virus infect-
ion would make it impracticable. The current United States and British policy is
to renounce the use of biological agents, while continuing research into defensive
measures against them.

SUMMARY

The threat of nuclear and chemical warfare remains and the strongest hope for
its prevention lies in deterrence. If the deterrent fails, soldiers are equipped
and trained to survive to continue the battle. There remains a possibility that
bacteriological warfare could be used on a strategic scale if it were thought to
be controllable, which is doubtful, but it is most unlikely that a tactical use is
feasible or as effective as other methods of waging war.

SELF TEST QUESTIONS

Question 1   What are the main three damaging effects from a nuclear explosion?

Answer ....

....

....

Question 2   In what ways would damage be caused by the blast wave?

Answer ....

....

....

....

....

Question 3   In what ways do the thermal effects of a nuclear blast cause damage?

Answer ....

....

....

Question 4   What types of radiation are there?

Answer ....

....

....

....

Question 5   What radiation doses would cause incapacitation among men? Give an indication of the extent.

Answer ....

....

Question 6   What are the tactical effects of residual radiation?

              Answer ....

              ....

Question 7   Which of the three main nuclear effects, from the following devices
              will cause damage over the greatest area to men in the open?

              a   A 1 KT airburst   ....

              b   A 150 KT airburst   ....

Question 8   Which of the three main nuclear effects from the following devices
              will cause damage over the greatest area to men in tanks?

              a   A 1 KT airburst   ....

              b   A 150 KT airburst   ....

Question 9   What are the tactical uses of:

              a   Persistent chemical agents?   ....

              ....

              ....

              b   Non-persistent chemical agents?   ....

              ....

              ....

Question 10   What prophylactic and therapeutic devices are there to counter
              nerve agents?

              Answer ....

              ....

ANSWERS ON PAGE 179

5
Small Arms and Cannons

INTRODUCTION

Of all weapons, small arms are the most numerous, the most commonly used and the best understood. This is because they are within the capability of almost everyone to operate and, up to the size of a rifle, can be used by civilians for sport and competition. Conversely, amongst military circles, cannons appear to be almost the least understood: perhaps because they lie between the well understood small arms and the more dramatic artillery guns. Nevertheless they play an important part in army units on reconnaissance vehicles, as air defence weapons and increasingly on MICVs. This chapter will assume that the term cannon covers weapons of 20 mm to 35 mm calibre. But first we will look at small arms.

SMALL ARMS

Although muskets in the form of matchlocks and flintlocks were used in the middle ages and rifles appeared in armies in the eighteenth century, it was not until the industrial revolution that small arms became more lethal than a longbow and arrow in the hands of a good archer. However, between the era of the Napoleonic wars, when muskets were still in common army use, and 1871, improved manufacturing methods resulted in a huge leap forward. At the end of that period, rifles such as the Martini-Henry were capable of accurate fire out to several hundreds of yards. In the latter half of the nineteenth century machine guns were developed until in the 1914 - 18 war Medium Machine Guns (MMGs) dominated the battlefield. It was, largely, to overcome their effectiveness that the tank was designed.

During the 1939 - 45 war most nations equipped their smallest infantry sub-units, their sections or squads, with rifles and a Light Machine Gun (LMG). Their firepower was supplemented with medium or sustained fire machine guns. Currently Warsaw Pact and NATO nations are either re-equipping with new families of small arms or considering doing so.

Before deciding what type of small arms should be adopted, it may be worthwhile to spend time deciding what is required of them in a modern war.

Fig. 1 Vickers MMG in use with The Manchester Regiment in Burma in
the 1939 - 45 war

The Task

Small arms are primarily anti-personnel weapons, though it is possible to damage
soft skinned vehicles, the optics of AFVs or even helicopters and aircraft with
well aimed or sustained fire.

During the Boer war the legend was created of the damage wreaked by marksmen
at vast ranges. There may have been some fine individual marksmen but the record from that war gives the figure of 3,000 rounds fired for each casualty inflic-
ted. By the 1914 - 18 war, the standard of marksmanship by the "Contemptibles"
was probably the highest ever achieved by the British Army. The effectiveness
of that army of long time professionals, before they were submerged by the huge
numbers of volunteers and conscripts who came after them, certainly impressed
the Germans. The Germans themselves quote a figure of 5,000 rounds fired for
each casualty in that war. Estimates in the 1939 - 45 war and in Korea give
10,000 rounds per casualty. These figures are by no means certain, but they
give an indication and they are not very surprising when a study of minor tactics

is made: most bullets are fired in a neutralising or suppressive role, giving covering fire for movement and winning the fire fight.

Another interesting way to look at figures, is to look at the percentage of total casualties caused by small arms fire. In 1870 the German casualties in the Franco-Prussian war were estimated as 91% from small arms fire and 9% from artillery fire. Between August 1914 and January 1917 the same figures for German casualties were 51% and 49%. United States figures in the 1941 - 45 war show an interesting trend. They assessed their percentages of casualties from small arms fire to be 30.7% in the Pacific where the war was largely fought by infantry, 23.4% in Europe where it was fought by a mixture of tanks and infantry, but only 14.0% in the Mediterranean where armoured forces were predominant. *

In Korea there are indications that possibly because of the bias towards infantry warfare, the percentage of casualties caused by small arms increased to 34%. It is difficult to judge from this data what the effects will be in any future conflict, particularly in Europe. It may be that if the increase in the numbers and effect-iveness of anti-armour weapons and the increased lethality of tank guns against other tanks continues, then there is a good chance that armoured forces can be stopped. Then infantry will be pushed forward to clear the way. At that stage intense small arms fire fights can be expected in which a large number of rounds will be fired.

Families of Small Arms

During and since the 1939 - 45 war the family of small arms in most armies has included pistols, sub machine guns (SMGs), rifles and machine guns. The term sub machine gun often causes confusion because it is not realised that it covers machine pistols - a German term, and carbines - an American term.

Pistols and SMGs are out of the main stream: they are for close quarter battle or self protection. The fire fight winning combination has been the rifle and machine gun. The differences have been that most nations have had rifles with an auto-matic capability whilst others, including the United Kingdom, have had single shot rifles; secondly some nations have had a Light Machine Gun (LMG) and Medium Machine Gun (MMG), while others have been equipped with a General Purpose Machine Gun (GPMG) to cover both roles.

Since the 1914 - 18 war the machine gun has been the main means of providing small arms neutralising or suppressive fire. Suppressive fire has been of two main types. One has been the provision of relatively long range, mainly defensive, fire and a large beaten zone with much the same role as artillery fire. In the case of the British Army it was provided throughout the 1914 - 18, 1939 - 45 and Korean wars by the Vickers MMG firing a .303 round (see Fig. 1). This gun, which had a water cooled barrel could provide sustained fire for as long as the ammunition could be produced. The German Army relied on its MG 42 (Spandau) which is still in use as the MG 3.

---

* The figures above were taken from RMCS Handbook of Infantry Weapons by
  Major F W Hobart.

Fig. 2 West German MG 3 GPMG

It was, and is, a GPMG. Its sustained rate of fire is made possible by a fairly
heavy barrel, which takes some time to heat up. The ability to change barrels
when the first one becomes too hot allows it to fire almost indefinitely.

The second requirement of the machine gun was to provide the main firepower
for the section or squad. The British Army had a LMG for this purpose for many
years, but when it changed over to 7.62 mm ammunition it adopted the GPMG
concept. The current GPMG, the L7A1, fills both the sustained fire role and the
section LMG role. To cope with sustained fire it has a changeable barrel. The
German Army continues to use its ubiquitous MG 3 in this role.

The Soviet Army has a family of Kalashnikov weapons. The MMG, which can be
used as a GPMG, fires a 7.62 mm bullet similar in size to the NATO standard,
but not in fact interchangeable. It is called the PK. The LMG is the RPK: it is
very lightweight, at 5 kg, and does not have an interchangeable barrel. It fires
the short Russian 7.62 mm round which is also used by the Russian AK 47.
Indeed, much of the RPK and AK 47 (see Fig. 3) are very similar: they strip down
in the same way and the RPK, in addition to its own 75 round drum magazine, can
use the AK 47 magazine. These similarities lead to a reduction of manufacturing
costs, commonality of spares, simple soldier training and simple logistic supply
to the section.

Fig. 3 Russian 7. 62 mm RPK and AKM (version of the AK 47)

The Russian AK 47, and its more modern version the AKM rifle, is often called an assault rifle after the German description for a shorter weapon and it is probably the widest used weapon in history. It has been made in huge numbers by many Eastern bloc nations. It is a well made weapon, robust and reliable. It is simple to operate and although its barrel length and muzzle velocity are less than Western rifles, its accuracy out to 300 m is not all that much less in the hands of an average soldier. It may not have the range, the accuracy or the stopping power of Western rifles, but perhaps it has enough.

In service Western rifles like the German G 3, the Belgian FN, including the British SLR derivative, and American M 14 are more powerful rifles, heavier, firing a bullet with a higher lethality further. Now most Western nations are considering a smaller, lighter weapon which will have a similar effective range to the AKM. The British are taking the family similarity even further by considering the adoption of a rifle, named an Individual Weapon (IW) and a LMG, named a Light Support Weapon (LSW) which have a great deal of commonality, fire the

same round and use the same magazines. For the first time, too, the British
Army is considering adopting an automatic capability on its rifle, or IW, which
has been common amongst most other nations for the past twenty years; until now
the British concept has been to fire accurate single shots in order to conserve
ammunition.

Not only NATO nations are adopting smaller weapon, recently a smaller Russian
rifle has been seen in Red Square.

Basic Design Balances

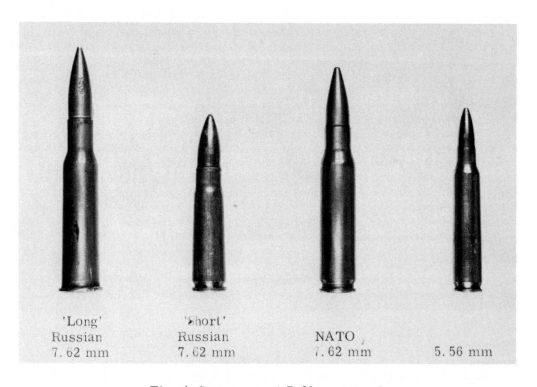

'Long'   'Short'
Russian   Russian   NATO
7.62 mm   7.62 mm   7.62 mm   5.56 mm

Fig. 4 Some current 7.62 mm rounds

Throughout history, the diameter or calibre of the rifle round has been steadily
reducing. Currently the most common calibre in the world is 7.62 mm but
various lengths and designs are in service, some of which are shown in Fig. 4.

The reduction in size has been made possible by an increase in muzzle velocity
thus maintaining the overall energy of the round. There is, however, a limit to
the amount that the mass or weight of the bullet can be reduced and it is tied up in
the design dilemma:

Design dilemma

Increase:	Decrease:
Accuracy	Weight
Range	Types of weapon
Lethality	Types of round
Reliability	Training time
Ease of operation	Maintenance time

The first part of the dilemma is to reduce the weight of the round and the weapon whilst increasing the accuracy, range, and lethality. If the weight of the round is reduced, then the range and penetration of cover is reduced unless the muzzle velocity is increased to compensate. When the United States introduced their Armalite 5. 56 mm rifle, the M 16, they reduced the weight of the round to approximately half that of the 7. 62 mm NATO round, from 25 g to 12 g and raised the muzzle velocity from 838 m sec to 990 m sec which means that it has approximately two thirds of the energy of a 7. 62 mm NATO bullet when it leaves the muzzle. So for half the weight a reduction of only one third in range and penetration has been achieved.

There is, however, a further advantage. Because the muzzle energy of the round is less the weight of the rifle can be less, too. In fact the M 16 weighs only 3.1 kg compared with the SLR's 4. 36 kg: so there is a further reduction in weight, again by nearly one third. Many advantages accrue from this reduction not the least being a reduction of the soldier's load; but in addition a lighter weapon is quicker into the aim and there is less recoil when it is fired. The last advantage bears fruit in making easier the training of recruits. It remains that the range is reduced, but that may not be very important.

Some American data accumulated from the 1939 - 45 war, Korea and Vietnam and shown in Fig. 5 shows the percentage of rifle engagements which occur within particular ranges.

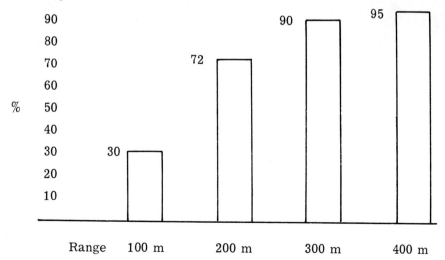

Fig. 5 Rifle engagement ranges

From the figures it perhaps could be deduced that a rifle with an effective range of 300 m to 400 m would be satisfactory. If this is agreed then it is possible to accept a lighter round and a lighter rifle. In general, NATO nations are accepting this compromise. A 5.56 mm rifle is sufficiently accurate, has sufficient range and has sufficient lethality at normal rifle combat ranges. It also decreases training time because it is easier to teach a recruit to shoot with a lighter rifle which is quicker into the aim and has less kick. Referring back to the design dilemma, there is no reason why, by accepting a lighter rifle, the ease of oper- ation will be changed or that maintenance time will be increased. So this leaves the decrease in the types of weapon and type of round.

Fig. 6 British Individual Weapon (IW)

From Fig. 6 it can be seen that the proposed British IW is a much smaller handier weapon than in the past, not only does this make it suitable for jumping in and out of armoured vehicles, but, with its automatic capability it is a very useful weapon for urban fighting. It combines the advantages of a SMG with the ability to fire accurately at longer ranges. It is also small enough to provide a personal defence weapon for headquarter staffs, AFV crews and logistic troops, at the same time giving them a better capability to defend their areas than they now have. It appears sensible, therefore, to replace the SMG and its 9 mm ammunition with the same small weapon which replaces the rifle. Such an answer removes the last of the design dilemmas; we have reduced the requirement by one type of weapon and one type of ammunition.

The next problem is to see if the reduction in types of weapon and ammunition can be carried through into the light machine gun field, but it is not possible to consider this in isolation. We must return to the inter-relationship of the family of small arms represented in the present generation by the rifle, LMG and MMG roles.

The Modern Machine Gun

As was mentioned earlier the machine gun has been the main method of providing suppressive fire from small arms. The MMG provided the sustained fire required in defence and in attack, often firing over the attacker's heads. The LMG provided sufficient suppressive fire for defence, to cover movement during the attack and to provide the bulk of section fire to win the fire fight.

The main requirements from the family of small arms are sufficient volume of fire to keep enemy heads down in the final assault or to win a fire fight and sufficient sustained fire for serious defensive battle or giving suppressive fire in the attack. When considering these requirements it is important to make allowance for the fact that a modern infantry section must also be armed to face armoured attack, so the number of men left operating small arms is reduced. There are several combinations of weapons which can provide the answer and three are well worth considering.

Fig. 7 Israeli 5.56 mm Galil

The first is to provide all those members of the section who fire small arms with the same weapon, halfway between a rifle and a LMG. A good modern example of this is the Galil (Fig. 7) which is a 5. 56 mm weapon with a bipod. Such a weapon can provide a good overall volume of fire from a section, but not sustained fire because with its fixed and light weight barrel it will overheat quite quickly. It will also not be very handy in confined areas like buildings or armoured vehicles because its overall length is 979 mm compared with the British IW length of 770 mm: it is perhaps with this in mind that Israel has produced a short barrelled version of the Galil with a folding butt. To back up such light weapons of restricted range, penetration of cover and sustained fire, it would be essential to have GPMGs in the platoon or company. In mechanised infantry such support would be easy, because a MG could be on each APC/MICV and it is easier to carry extra weapons and ammunition. In non-mechanised units it would not be so easy.

The second solution is to have a light weight rifle and a GPMG in each section. West Germany tends towards this solution. Certainly they are unhappy to change their GPMG, the MG 3. Their experience in fighting the Russian Army has led them to keep this 7. 62 mm GPMG which, with its changeable barrel, can not only sustain its fire for long periods but can produce a very high rate of fire of 1, 200 rounds per minute, nearly twice the normal rate. With such a section mix of weapons the drawback would be that two types of ammunition, 5. 56 mm and 7. 62 mm, would be required with a resultant loss in flexibility and an increase in logistic complexity. In addition the relatively heavy GPMG and 7. 62 mm ammunition would need to be humped in the section.

The third solution is that which the Russians have adopted in the last generation and which is now being considered by the British Army. It consists of a light weight weapon, an IW, and a very similar one, a LSW with a heavier barrel and a bipod. Some of the advantages of this system are:

a The ammunition and magazines are completely interchangeable with the consequent logistic advantage.

b The weight of weapons and ammunition in the section is drastically reduced.

c The training is simplified.

Perhaps another advantage is that if the requirement for a GPMG to be light enough to be carried in the section no longer exists, then it can be made with heavier barrels to improve its sustained fire capability. The big disadvantage of this section mix is the same as for the Galil system: a GPMG back-up is required in the platoon or company to provide range, penetration of cover and sustained fire.

The main factor which decides which family of small arms to adopt is the role envisaged for it. The most demanding will be in the hands of the infantry and the main question is the requirement for sustained fire. Any weapon will overheat in time unless it can be cooled. It is worth spending some time considering this aspect.

Heating in Small Arms

In the past a very efficient cooling system was to employ water in a jacket around the barrel as in the Vickers MMG used in the 1914 - 18 and 1939 - 45 wars. It is not feasible for a more portable GPMG or LMG. Even the finning of barrels, rather like that on a motor cycle engine, helps very little unless a strong wind is blowing. It is not worth the extra weight.

Recent tests show that any barrel heats up above an acceptable limit after a time. The heat produces three main problems: the weapon becomes too hot to handle, then the chamber becomes hot enough to cook off any round left in there and finally the barrel becomes so hot that the metal softens slightly and wears very quickly. The last phenomenon, in common shooting terms, results in a shot out barrel and the bullets tumble or key-hole a few metres after leaving the muzzle. Designs can solve the cook off problem by not allowing a round to be chambered until just before it is fired: this is achieved by the moving parts being held back in the 'open bolt' position until the trigger is pulled. The working parts then move forward, pick up the round, chamber it and fire it. Most machine guns avoid the very high temperatures at which barrels wear quickly by having changeable barrels. The current British GPMG, the Bren Gun and the new (Fabrique Nationale) FN Minimi LMG all have changeable barrels. One exception to the rule is the Russian RPK: it has a fixed barrel and will probably reach cook off temper- ature, firing at 50 rounds per minute, soon after five minutes. The FN Minimi could carry on with its changeable barrel at the same rate almost indefinitely.

The problems caused by a changeable barrel are greater weight, an extra 2, 1 kg above the 6. 5 kg in the case of the Minimi, and more training required for the user. The West German Army still clings to its proven MG 3, firing 7. 62 mm ammunition, with its changeable barrel. Moreover it retains its high cyclic rate of fire at 1, 200 rounds per minute, compared with most GPMG or LMG rates which are in the bracket of 500 - 1, 000 rounds per minute. The need for such a high rate of fire is based on the belief that a very high cyclic rate of fire will cause high casualties before enemy soldiers can get to ground.

The heating problem makes the adoption of light-weight weapons difficult. The user needs to decide where his compromise lies between his desire for a light weight weapon and his need for sustained fire: he must decide whether or not he is prepared to carry a second barrel and he must decide whether the accuracy he requires really is such that he must demand a closed bolt, so risking a cook off.

Automatic Fire from Rifles

Except for sniping, it is unlikely that any new rifle will be adopted into military service without an automatic capability. It will herald the end of an era for the British Army which has believed in restrained accurate single round fire: a con- cept which led, in the present generation of small arms to the deliberate exclusion of the automatic capability from the SLR, even though other nations adopted the same weapon with it.

Recent British Army experience against forces equipped with the Russian auto- matic AK 47 has led to a belief that the greater volume of fire available from automatic rifles is essential to win the fire fight. On the other hand, an inexperienced soldier, even though well trained, may well, in the excitement of his first combat experience shoot off his ammunition very quickly on automatic. Perhaps a way of preventing this is to incorporate a limited burst capability on the weapon. FN incorporate a three round limited burst capability in addition to single round and automatic on their 5.56 mm CAL rifle. They also incorporate a three to six round capability on their Minimi LMG.

Apart from the conservation of ammunition, the limited burst capability enables a user to re-aim between each burst. Such adjustment is important because rifles, without bipods, or SMGs, pull upwards to such an extent that, even at 25 m, firers are unable to keep more than three rounds on a four foot square target. There is certainly a case for a limiting device but the penalty would be some extra time to train a soldier to use a change lever with more choices.

Accuracy and Sighting

Accuracy is a combination of a good sighting system and a skilled firer. First, however, the weapon itself must be consistent, which means that, when fired from a firmly clamped weapon, the rounds will be tightly grouped. Consistency demands that there must be as little variation between the manufacture and make up of each round as possible. Batches of rounds vary and to give an idea of the spread of consistency from batch to batch the British acceptance limit is that the average distance of hits from the mean point of impact (mpi) should not exceed 8"; but one of the best batches produced in Britain averaged 2.8". It is interest- ing to note that a perfect shot, using ammunition at the 8" acceptance limit, allow- ing for no human error in range or wind estimation, has only approximately a 92% chance of hitting a man at 400 m, 71% at 600 m and 54% at 800 m. In reality, when weather effects and human error are taken into account, an average shot has much less chance of a hit than these figures indicate.

Jump and other movements of the gun after the trigger has been pulled are the main reasons for lack of consistency in the weapon itself. Jump can be reduced by designing a well balanced weapon and by having a heavy weapon which will absorb the recoil and cut down the kick to the firer: the extreme case of this can be seen in the heavy .22 match rifles. With larger calibre weapons the weight cannot be used to much advantage because it then becomes too heavy for the firer to sustain a steady hold and carry about, so it behoves the designer to produce a well balanced weapon with a consistent jump.

Once consistency has been achieved, accuracy becomes only a matter of adjusting the mpi over the target. This is done by aligning the line from the muzzle of the weapon to the target with the line from the eye through the sighting system to the target.

An open sight or an aperture sight means that the firer must align the target, the foresight and the back sight. A little luck must be involved because it is not pos- sible to focus on all three at once. There is some evidence to show that the task is made easier in an aperture sight by the natural ability of the eye to place the foresight in the middle of the backsight aperture without fine focussing: it may be that the eye seeks the brightest point, which is the middle. Obviously the longer the sight base, the more accurate the sighting.

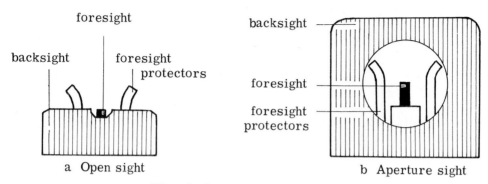

a Open sight   b Aperture sight

Fig. 8 Open and aperture sights

The problem of focussing on three objects can be removed in an optical sight. It
is demonstrated with the aid of Fig. 9.

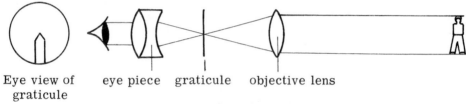

Eye view of   eye piece   graticule   objective lens
  graticule

Fig. 9 Optical sight

The target is focussed on to a plate on which is etched a foresight. The point of
the foresight is in the middle of the optical field of view. This leaves the firer's
eye only to focus itself on to the plate which in Britain is called a graticule and in
the United States a reticle. (Optical experts will note that the erector lens is ex-
cluded from Fig. 9. This is for simplicity). It is much easier and even an optical system with no magnification makes aiming easier. An optical system which
magnifies assists accuracy and it also assists the firer to see his target more
clearly in poor light conditions such as dawn, dusk and even at night when it is
not very dark and overcast. A problem with an optical sight is that it slows down
the firer's time to come into the aim. It can be seen, too, that the higher the
magnification, the smaller will be the field of view and the slower will be the time
to come into the aim because it takes longer to locate the target in the sight.
Once again there can not be an advantage without a compensating disadvantage.

The more important drawbacks to an optical sight are its size, weight, bulk and
cost: for example the Sight Unit Small Arms Trilux (SUSAT) sight on the proposed
British IW, with its attaching bracket, weighs approximately $\frac{1}{2}$ kg and is expensive. It stands up high off the weapon and is a little vulnerable.

A sighting system which helps many firers to come into the aim quickly is the
Single Point sight, with which the firer keeps both eyes open.

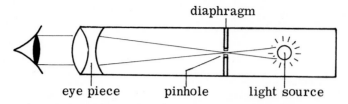

Fig. 10 Principle of a Single Point sight

A light source is placed at the focus of an eye-piece lens with the result that one of the firer's eyes sees a spot of light at infinity. With his other eye he views the target. When he has aligned the spot of light with the target the aim is achieved.

Caseless Ammunition

Ever since small arms adopted cartridge cases in the mid nineteenth century to give good breech sealing and remove much of the heat from the breech, the return to caseless ammunition has been contemplated. The advantage would be very much lighter ammunition, probably it would be one quarter the weight of the current 7.62 mm NATO round. Unfortunately the original reasons for adopting the cased round still exist; a case provides good breech sealing, removes much heat when it is ejected, protects the propellant from weather, holds the propellant together and prevents its chance ignition.

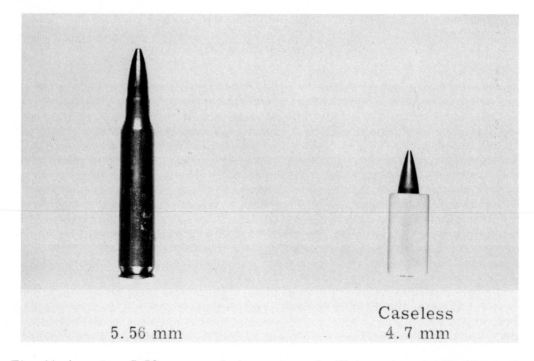

Fig. 11 American 5.56 mm round size compared with experimental Heckler and Koch 4.7 mm caseless round

The West German firm of Heckler and Koch are experimenting with a weapon which fires a 4.75 mm caseless round, their G 11. It has gone a long way to solving many of the problems created by caseless ammunition and we may yet see a caseless system in the next generation of rifles. One of its rounds, compared with the United States 5.56 mm round used in the Armalite rifle, is shown in Fig. 11. Whereas the 5.56 mm round is half the weight of a 7.62 mm NATO round, the caseless round is half that weight again; so the advantages which would accrue to the heavily loaded infantryman would be impressive.

BAYONETS

Traditionalists would never forgive the omission of some mention of bayonets. Although they were used in anger in the Far East during the 1939 - 45 war, it is difficult to find a record of their use in Western Europe. On the other hand there is no doubt that they were often fixed during that war, the Korean war and since. The fixing of bayonets is more than a fixing of steel to a rifle it puts iron into the soul of the soldier doing the fixing.

Modern small rifles or IW are not very well suited to bayonets nor are they likely to be strong enough to stand the violent use of a bayonet fixed to them. But then perhaps a bayonet is an emotive rather than a seriously practical weapon?

VEHICLE MACHINE GUNS

Surprisingly, until recent years, not much effort has been put into the development of specialised vehicle machine guns. Generally they have been adapted from MGs designed for the ground role. A good example of this is the adaptation of the British L7A2 GPMG to be a L8A1 fitted in the Chieftain tank: it entailed a considerable modification.

In deciding what sort of vehicle MG to fit, first we must decide what we want the MG to do. The most accepted requirement is to engage infantry in the open, provide suppressive fire and to engage soft vehicles. A 7.62 mm MG can satisfy all these needs. It can be argued that it is also desirable to be able to engage lightly armoured vehicles like the Russian BMP with a MG: such a requirement would demand a 12.7 mm weapon to be capable of inflicting some damage and a 25 mm cannon to be sure of defeating the frontal armour. In the future, as armoured protection improves, a larger cannon will be required. The main practical disadvantage in accepting a larger calibre is the greater volume of storage space required for the very much larger rounds: rounds for cannons are large and should be referred to as shells. Consequently most modern tanks have MGs with a calibre near to 7.62 mm though a rare exception is the French AMX 30 tank which has a co-axially mounted 20 mm cannon.

The design of an AFV MG should ensure that it does not protrude from the armour so much that it is vulnerable to small arms or artillery fire. It should also not extend far into the turret space because that space is at a premium. Despite this it should be simple to change the barrels when they become hot, and they should be capable of being withdrawn rearwards. Finally the fumes from the breech should not discharge into the turret space. A purpose built vehicle MG can achieve these design requirements to a large extent.

A possible advantage a vehicle MG can possess over its ground based counterpart is a power driven ammunition feed system, as has frequently been the case on aircraft mounted weapons. The American Vulcan 20 mm cannon and the 7.62 mm minigun are both examples of power driven weapons which, as a result, can produce a very high rate of fire. More recently the Hughes Chain Gun has been developed in the United States. It has a motor which drives a chain similar to that used on a bicycle; the chain is used to drive the feed and all the working parts, so they do not depend upon gas operation. The overall result is a very reliable system. The drawback is its reliance on a power source: again only the user can decide for himself if he will risk his MG being out of action if the power source fails.

Fig. 12   Hughes 7.62 mm Chain Gun

CANNONS

Increasingly cannons are being power driven. Cannons have been used in aircraft and on ships in large numbers, but they have been rare in military equipments until comparatively recently when their use on Reconnaissance Vehicles, Mechanised Infantry Combat Vehicles and as anti-aircraft weapons has proliferated. Their main use in modern warfare is to destroy lightly armoured vehicles, soft vehicles and aircraft but they are also useful against other point targets.

An important decision to be taken by the soldier is whether the role of the cannon is to be primarily anti-light armour or anti-aircraft. At their extremes the two roles demand different characteristics. One extreme is characterised by the British 30 mm Rarden gun. It was designed, at the British Army's request, primarily as an anti-APC weapon: it was particularly specified that the gun should be capable of defeating the thickest armour of an APC at battle ranges. To achieve such a performance a weapon must be accurate and leads the designer towards a single shot weapon: barrel vibration set up by automatic fire would reduce accuracy. The designer from the Royal Small Arms Factory at Enfield has met the requirement entirely. Anyone who has seen the Rarden's astonishing accuracy cannot but be impressed. It is capable of firing APDS, APSE (Armour Piercing Special Effect) and HE rounds.

Fig. 13 Rarden gun on Scimitar reconnaissance vehicle

The gun has, however, only a limited effectiveness against aircraft, including helicopters. For this role, the essential requirement from a gun is a high rate of fire. Such guns in the present day are normally fitted into complex air defence vehicle systems as is the American Vulcan 20 mm cannon. (See Fig. 14). It has a Gatling gun configuration with six barrels which are driven round. Its rate of fire can be adjusted to 1,000 rounds per minute or 3,000 rounds per minute. Even such high rates of fire do not guarantee a hit on an aircraft. To be a really effective air defence weapon system, a good target acquisition and lock-on capability is required to guide the weapon. In such a system the guns will amount only to approximately a fortieth or fiftieth of the cost of the total system.

Fig. 14 American 20 mm Vulcan gun

If, as is often the case, the user wishes the gun to be effective against lightly armoured vehicles and to provide a reasonable deterrence to low flying aircraft and helicopters, then a fully automatic cannon is probably the best compromise. The German MICV, the Marder mounts a 20 mm gun made by Rheinmetal to provide for both roles: it has a rate of fire up to 1,000 rounds per minute and can be aimed upwards at an angle of 1,080 mil (60°) when required. It would be wrong to say that such a concept is likely to shoot down FGA or even helicopters very effectively, but it does provide a considerable deterrence, even though the bill is a high expenditure of ammunition.

There is little doubt that there are many reliable and effective cannons available with a range of rates of fire to suit all requirements. It is important for the soldier to realise that no cannon can be a jack of all trades and that he must be able to define his compromise carefully, so that the designer can provide as effective an answer as is possible.

SUB MACHINE GUNS

There are often misconceptions about this group of weapons: in Germany and Russia they are known as 'Machine Pistols', in the United States they are known as 'Machine Carbines' or just 'Carbines' and since the 1939 - 45 war when Hitler is credited with coining the phrase 'Assault Rifle', the confusion is even greater.

Fig. 15 Ingram SMG

Perhaps the confusion will disappear as modern rifles reduce in size and calibre but are given an automatic capability, and so to a great extent usurp the role of the SMG.

The role of a SMG is first of all self protection for those soldiers who are not expected to be involved in assault or defence: they are soldiers in headquarters, communications and vehicles such as tank crews. Secondly SMGs are very useful for close quarter combat as practised by commandos or by all infantry in urban fighting. These roles lead to a weapon which is light, handy, has a short range and an automatic capability. It does not need to be very accurate or have very much penetration.

The 5.56 mm rifles with an automatic capability can fulfil the traditional role in most cases. The exception is clandestine operations when the need is for a very small weapon similar to the Ingram which despite its length of only 248 mm has a rate of fire of approximately 1,200 rounds per minute.

Fig. 16 Heckler and Koch MP5K A1

Of similar concept is the more robust Heckler and Koch 9 mm MP5K AJ which
was designed for use by special police and anti-terrorist squads.

CONCLUSION

It is hoped that readers of this chapter have understood that although modern
advances in design and technology have allowed improvements in the design of
small arms and cannons, it is more important that the soldier thinks out very
carefully what function he wants his weapons to perform and what compromises
he is willing to accept to obtain what he is looking for.

SELF TEST QUESTIONS

Question 1   In what ways does the Russian short 7.62 mm round differ from
              the standard NATO 7.62 mm round?

              Answer ....

                      ....

                      ....

                      ....

Question 2   How is the stopping power of the lighter 5.56 mm round main-
              tained so that it does not drop too much below that of a 7.62 mm
              round?

              Answer ....

                      ....

Question 3   What are three options for the section family of weapons?

              Answer ....

                      ....

                      ....

Question 4   What are the practical effects on a rifle or LMG of overheating?

              Answer ....

                      ....

                      ....

Question 5   What are the advantages and disadvantages of providing an
              automatic capability on a rifle?

              Advantages ....

                          ....

              Disadvantages ....

                          ....

                          ....

Question 6   What is the difference between consistency and accuracy?

Answer ....

....

....

....

Question 7   What are the advantages and disadvantages of an optical sight
compared with an open sight?

Advantages ....

....

....

Disadvantages ....

....

....

....

....

Question 8   What are the extra problems encountered when fitting a MG into
an armoured vehicle?

Answer ....

....

....

Question 9   What is the main difference between a cannon designed specifically for Air Defence and one designed to attack lightly armoured
vehicles?

Answer ....

....

....

Question 10   What are the main roles for a SMG?

Answer   ....

....

ANSWERS ON PAGE   180

6

Command, Control and Communications (C³)

INTRODUCTION

In modern warfare, it is essential that a commander at any level can quickly assess the relative positions and strengths of both sides and the possible future actions of the enemy. His consequent plan of action must be passed to every man under his command and he must then be able to control the implementation of his plan by swift assimilation of the enemy's reactions, assessment of their effect-iveness and adjustment of his own troops actions.

The facilities to perform these functions have always been basic components of an army but today they must be swifter in response, more comprehensive in cover-age and provide control at a much higher level than ever before. In the Victorian era commanders in the far flung corners of the world accrued vast tracts of con-tinents for the British Empire without the immediate knowledge or even intention of the British Parliament. By the time of the Vietnam war, the President of the United States was able to talk directly to a soldier locked in combat; and in the case of the American attempt to rescue the hostages from Iran, to exercise direct control, from Washington, of a force in a Middle Eastern desert. If a future major East-West conflict were to erupt, the communications required to allow the international consultation at head of government level to co-ordinate their armed forces reactions at each stage of escalation in the conflict will need to be instant and reliable. Interestingly, one of the most reliable links required will be that which allows heads of state of opposing sides to confer, to prevent mutual destruction.

It is against this background that military communications must be considered and this chapter will consider the communications from the FEBA backwards. First, however, it is necessary to understand some basic elements of communication.

BASIC CONCEPTS

The Communication Spectrum

Any electromagnetic wave travels through space or the atmosphere at a speed of 300,000,000 metres per second (m/sec), so for any given wavelength we can work out the number of waves a second passing a point: this is the frequency and is measured in Hertz (Hz). For example a 300 m long wave will have a frequency of $\dfrac{300,000,000}{300m}$ m/sec = 1,000,000 Hertz per second. For ease of reference the following abbreviations are used:

1 Gigahertz (GHz) = 1,000,000,000 Hz
1 Megahertz (MHz) = 1,000,000 Hz
1 Kilohertz (KHz) = 1,000 Hz

1 pico metre (p)   = $\dfrac{1}{1,000,000,000,000}$ m

The wave lengths of frequencies used in communication are those in the Electro-magnetic Spectrum below those of the infra-red. This is shown diagrammatically in Fig. 1.

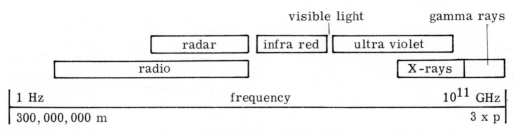

Fig. 1 Electromagnetic system

One final basic piece of shorthand which it is necessary to explain is the classi-fication of radio frequencies into 'bands'. These are:

Low Frequency (LF)	30	– 300 KHz
Medium Frequency (MF)	300 KHz	– 3 MHz
High Frequency (HF)	3	– 30 MHz
Very High Frequency (VHF)	30	– 300 MHz
Ultra High Frequency (UHF)	300 MHz	– 3 GHz
Super High Frequency (SHF)	3	– 30 GHz
Extra High Frequency (EHF)	30	– 300 GHz

Bandwidth

Bandwidth, so far as communication is concerned, is the amount of the spectrum taken up by a communication channel, and probably the width of that channel is the simplest way to regard it. The fact is that although we tune in a receiver or transmitter to a particular frequency, say 300 MHz, we are, in reality, tuning into the centre of a band of frequencies. Thus a channel needs a considerable amount of frequency space, free from interference, if good communications are to be achieved. The problem is that so many channels, military and civilian, are required that there is considerable competition for the frequency space available. For this reason communication channels are spreading further and further into SHF and EHF bands. Obviously the narrower the bandwidth of a channel can be made, the more channels can be fitted in. The following table gives an indication of the bandwidth of channels required for different types of communication in military systems:

Morse	– 150	Hz
Teleprinter	– 150	Hz
Computer data	– 150	Hz
Facsimile (a copy of a form /table /map)	– 1, 500	Hz (but normally use an available voice channel)
HF voice (AM)	– 3 - 6	KHz
VHF - EHF voice (FM)	– 20	KHz
Television	– 5. 5	MHz

When designing a communication system, the allowance for bandwidth is an essential feature. For example the spacing between channels on the new Clansman VHF radios is 25 KHz, which makes sense when the 20 KHz bandwidth required for a VHF channel is considered. The 5.5 MHz bandwidth required by a television channel also explains why it is not used widely in military communications: a television channel would take up the same space as approximately two hundred and fifty voice channels.

It is now time to look at the various types of communications starting from the FEBA and working backwards.

NET RADIO

Most forward units and formations use the flexible net radio system with all the stations able to move at will with no interruption in communications. To understand the various advantages of HF and VHF radio nets it is useful to know the main characteristics of HF (3 - 30 MHz) and VHF (30 - 300 MHz).

HF Characteristics

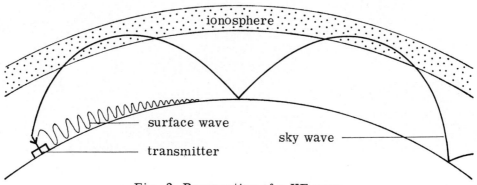

Fig. 2 Propagation of a HF wave

HF waves are, by military radio communication standards, very long: a 15 MHz wave is 20 m long. It travels both along the surface of the ground or by refraction in the ionosphere which is a series of layers of ionised air molecules between 50 km and 500 km above the surface of the earth. The refraction is enough to bend waves in the HF band back to earth to form what is known as a skywave.

Fig. 2 shows the skywave skipping from the earth to the ionosphere and back again. Such a method of communication allows very long distances to be covered

Fig. 3 PRC-320 HF set

and it is possible to communicate around the world using HF. It also, in its wake, produces the main drawback of HF communication: stations from great distances away can interfere with what is intended to be a local radio link. At night, and around dusk and dawn in particular, HF frequencies become very noisy and suffer severe interference because the ionosphere moves up and down and changes in strength. Fading of the signal strength also occurs for the same reasons.

The surface wave can, to a certain extent, hug the earth's surface, and so achieve a good range of communication. Its ability to do this is enhanced because such relatively long waves can bend round obstructions and pass through them more easily than the shorter VHF waves. The range of the radio link depends much upon the power of the transmitting end and the sensitivity of the receiving end. As an indication of the distances achieved, the British Clansman HF radio, the manpack PRC-320, has a range of 50 km by surface wave and 300 km by skywave.

From its characteristics it can be seen that HF is very useful for sets which re-quire a long range and for use in urban, jungle or very mountainous regions where its ability to bend round obstacles would be useful. On the other hand it is noisy and subject to interference to an extent where it may be unusable at night for voice communication. Because the wavelength affects the length of the antennas, the relatively long HF wavelength demands a relatively long antenna.

VHF Characteristics

VHF wavelengths are shorter: for example at 150 MHz, in the middle of the band, a radio wave is 2 m long. Also, because more bandwidth is available, Frequency Modulation (FM) can be used instead of the Amplitude Modulation (AM) used in HF sets. It is in fact the AM modulation which permits the narrow bandwidth of approximately 3 - 6 KHz as opposed to about 20 KHz required for FM modulation. However, FM brings with it less noise and interference by day and night, small antennas, better speech quality and a 'capture effect' which is made possible because FM radios can home in on the strong required signal while suppressing the unwanted weaker signals which would cause interference.

The shorter VHF wavelengths are not so good at bending around obstacles as their longer brothers in the HF band. Also they are often reflected off obstacles. This can cause difficulties in wooded or urban areas in particular: the reflections often cause confusing conditions in which reception can be zero in one spot but strong one or two paces away.

The short waves do not follow the curvature of the earth so well as HF waves. When this is coupled with the weakening effect caused by obstacles, it can be seen that the range of VHF communication is inherently much shorter than HF. The Clansman VHF man-pack PRC-352 set has a range of approximately 16 km and the vehicle borne VRC-353 has a range of 30 km.

On the other hand VHF FM sets can easily be put 'back to back' to re-broadcast the signal and thus increase the range. Such a technique is very useful in hilly or urban conditions.

Fig. 4 PRC-352 VHF set

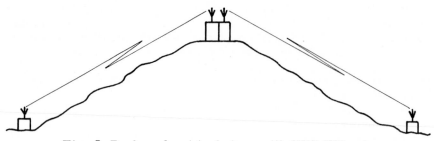

Fig. 5 Re-broadcast technique with VHF FM sets

Military Net Radios

Soldiers demand much from their military net radios. The British Clansman system is a good example of well thought out military net radios. Whenever possible they have common design features which allow:

    a The interchange between sets of audio gear, batteries and battery charging which simplifies the logistic backing.

    b Common operating techniques which cut down the training time for operators.

c Simplified and common maintenance features which not only reduce training time but also reduce repair time.

d Interoperability which permits stations using different sets to talk together on the same net (see frequency overlap in Annex to this chapter).

e Different sets to be used in the same vehicle without interfering with each other.

f Their use in all parts of the world in rugged conditions.

To achieve these advantages costs money and any military radio is by commercial standards very expensive indeed. Also because of the severe testing required it takes a considerable time to develop, so in the rapidly advancing electronic world, a new military radio is not necessarily using the very latest technology available. Commercial radio can adapt new technology much more quickly.

Commercial Net Radio

Fig. 6 The VRC 391 vehicle commercial set

Commercial net radio can be used in situations where the rigorous conditions, for which military radios are designed, do not exist. Internal Security (IS) situations and guarding large areas such as airfields or storage depots are examples. The radios can be small and work on small power supplies if a central booster station with its associated well sited antenna can be used. In such a case very small pocket and vehicle borne sets can be used over a wide area. The current sets in use by the British Army are the body worn radio PRC-392 and the vehicle borne VRC-391.

The use of the relatively cheap commercial sets instead of military sets, where possible, results in a considerable capital saving.

TRUNK COMMUNICATIONS

In forward units VHF net radios with a limited range provide satisfactory immediate communications and the stations can be very mobile. In addition the short range of the sets and the immediate nature of the messages do not allow enemy intercept stations to receive, or if they do to have time to act on, the information received. Communication between formations requires long links and the information, such as operational orders, is not so immediate that an enemy Electronic Warfare (EW) system could not take action on it. For these reasons net radio communications are not suitable and from Brigade Headquarters rearwards it is normal for trunk communications to be used. Like the formations they serve, trunk communications are less mobile and flexible than net radio communications and the units they serve. On the other hand they can provide not only open voice communication but secure voice, teleprinter, computer data and facsimile channels. Television channels are theoretically possible, but they are normally only used within a large formation headquarters with cable connections because of the wide 5.5 MHz bandwidth they take up.

Command and Trunk Communications

Throughout the 1939 - 45 war, armies exercised command through communications which followed the chain of command down through the headquarters as in Fig. 7.

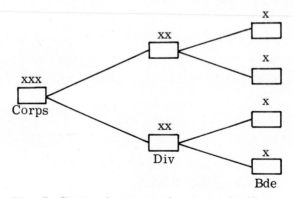

Fig. 7 Chain of command communications

Heavy duty multi-core cables were used until the advent of A10 Radio Relay (RR) which was used by Field Marshal Montgomery to communicate from his head-quarters to the United Kingdom during the advance from Normandy through to Germany in 1944 - 45.

Radio relay is a radio link which uses VHF, UHF or SHF because these frequency bands allow more bandwidth for each channel. Because it uses short waves, the link is little more than line of sight otherwise the signal is absorbed by obstruct-ions, but this in itself makes it difficult to intercept if it is carefully sited.

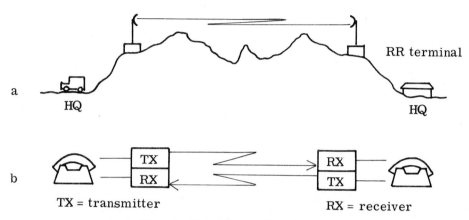

Fig. 8 Principles of radio relay

In Fig. 8a the link between the two sets replaces the old cable system. The use of directional antennas means that a very narrow radio beam is used ensuring that the risk of interference and interception is further reduced and a strong signal can be created with minimum of power.

If a chain of command system were adopted using radio relay, the three problems created would be first the creation of large joint communications and headquarter complex which would be difficult to conceal, secondly a very difficult siting pro-blem because of the need to put antennas on hills and thirdly a vulnerable com-munication network, which would be broken if an intermediate headquarter communications, such as division, were put out of action or changed location. To cure all these problems communications centres (Comcens) were developed sep-arate from headquarters, so the expanded chain of command system was created:

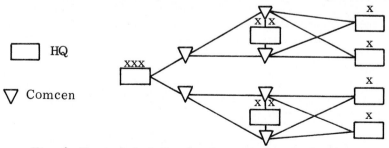

Fig. 9 Expanded chain of command communication

Radio relay links are provided between Comcens and from the Comcens to the headquarter locations. A study of the system will show that some Comcens and headquarters can be put out of action without disrupting the whole communication system. The headquarters can now also be sited and camouflaged well away from high ground. This is the stage to which communications have currently been developed in European armies: in the British Army the system goes under the general name of Bruin.

By the nature of the links, the terminals are sited on high ground and must there-fore be obvious targets. Consequently it is possible that even an expanded chain of command communication system may be put out of action. Following such a logic most NATO nations are considering the use of area systems of communica-tions: the American system is 'Tritac', France is developing 'Rita', Germany is fielding 'Autoko' and the United Kingdom is planning to bring 'Ptarmigan' into service in the middle 1980s. The principle is demonstrated in Fig. 10.

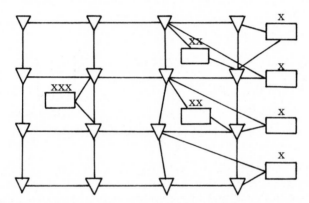

Fig. 10 Layout of an area communication system

In this case the Comcens have been replaced by a matrix of 'trunk nodes' which fulfil much the same function as Comcens but much else as well. The nodes cover the operational area and under reasonable communications conditions they can be sited from fifteen to twenty kilometres apart.

The central component of a node is a vehicle containing a computer controlled electronic switch. In effect it is an automatic exchange which searches for a clear route through the system when a subscriber is dialled and makes the con-nection. Around the switch vehicle are radio relay terminal vehicles which form the links to other trunk nodes, to headquarter locations, to flank formations or; in the case of Ptarmigan, to Single Channel Radio Access (SCRA) facilities.

A SCRA consists of a VHF radio on the end of a radio relay link from a trunk node. The VHF radio can also receive from and transmit messages to a mobile radio in a vehicle or carried by a man. As a result the mobile radio can use the whole area communications system.

There is no doubt that such a system will bring enormous advantages with its comparative invulnerability, its secure speech facility and its ability to provide voice, teleprinter, facsimile and computer data links.

Computers in Command Control and Communication

Modern computers in the form of microcomputers using microprocessors can be
fitted to carry out such functions as controlling washing machines and timing
internal combustion engines, or, in the form of large computers, they can be
much more complex like the system which controls all bookings worldwide for a
large airline. Already, as described before, there are computers to control the
routing of radio calls in modern military communication systems. They can also
be used to help staff officers and commanders at headquarters.

The United States is investigating the use of a computer system named 'Tactical
Operations System' (TOS), France is looking at its 'Sycomore' system and the
United Kingdom has been trying out its 'Wavell' system in BAOR. The concept of
Wavell is to store information, update it constantly and display it as required.
The basic up to date data is entered into the computer store before deployment.
The Wavell data during trials has been divided into the sections or formats shown
in Fig. 11.

OPERATIONS		INTELLIGENCE
FORMAT	FORMAT	FORMAT

Srl	Title	Srl	Title	Srl	Title
01	Unit data	12	Reserved areas	29	En contact report
02	Unit locs	16	Codeword list	30	ECR Summary
03	Combat Str (Div)	17	Codeword index	31	En unit data
04	Combat Str (Corps)	18	Codeword allocation	32	EUD Summary
05	ORBAT (Div)	19	Nuc strike Wng	33	En Fmn data
06	ORBAT (Corps)	20	Nickname list	34	En ORBAT
07	Organic HQ data	21	Nickname index	35	INTSUM
08	Summary of HQ locs	22	Nickname allocation	38	En AFV state
09	Reserved Dml	23	General purpose list	40	General purpose list
10	Res Dml Summary	24	SITREP	41	INTREP

Fig. 11 Computer formats used in Wavell trials

Commanders or staff officers can call up on the screen of a Visual Display Unit
(VDU) any one of the formats. An example is given in Fig. 12.

Each format is kept up-dated. At present, if required on a map, they must be
transferred by hand, but now development of projected maps and overlays which
can be automatically up-dated is under way. A paper print out of any of the formats can be provided quickly if required.

One of the greatest advantages is that the computer stores can up-date each other.
Assume that at each headquarters there is a computer for Main HQ and its temporary step up station used on moves; then all computers at all HQs can pass their

```
01 INPUT HQ  4DV     ENEMY CONTACT NO 05/0006
02
03 CONTACT  SOURCE      UNIT/FMN    LOCATION   EQPT  SEEN CAS  ACTIVITY
04  TIME
05 031742  21INFBN..  NOT KNOWN....  SQ877654  X32.... ..6 ..2  MOVE SW..
06                                              112APC. .12 ..4  .........
07                                              95SPGUN ..4 ...  .........
08                                              AD EQPT ..3 ..1  .........
09                                              ........ ... ...  .........
10                                              ........ ... ...  .........
11                                              ........ ... ...  .........
12
13
14
15 COMMENT   ...............................................................
16          ...............................................................
17          ...............................................................
18
19 ECR ASSD ...............................................................
20
PROMPTS:
ERRORS:
COMMANDS:‾
```

Fig. 12 Example of a Wavell format

up-dating of the same data to each other via data channels in Bruin or Ptarmigan or other modern communication systems. When a step up is established its computer store can be up-dated as soon as communications are established: anyone who has experienced the time consuming task of doing this by voice and writing the information down will readily realise the great step forward this is!

A summary of the advantages a command and control computer can provide is:

a A commander and his staff are kept up to date with the battle and can re-group their own formation more easily to react to the changing situation.

b A very quick transfer of command is possible.

c Print outs can eliminate many state-boards.

d The information contained in each computer store is the same and not corrupted by human error.

e Much radio communication traffic is replaced by computer data channels with a consequent reduction in time, effort and channel space.

f Many periodic returns become unnecessary because the formats are automatically kept up to date.

There is no doubt that trials to date have convinced commanders and staffs that command and control is considerably improved and speeded by the use of computers. It does not take much imagination to see that its extension to the logistic staff and control of the logistic chain could equally be of considerable benefit.

With the introduction of area communication systems like Ptarmigan and computer aided control systems like Wavell perhaps, for the first time since the innovation of the Blitzkrieg, commanders and their staffs will be able to read the battle sufficiently quickly to be able to influence it quickly. Such an ability is especially important in a defensive situation to enable rapid re-grouping to react against an attacker's breakthrough. If a modern command and control system is to keep functioning in an Electronic Warfare (EW) environment it must be able to withstand Radio Electronic Combat Support (RECS) assault. It is worth considering what are the implications.

ELECTRONIC WARFARE

Fig. 13 A direction finding equipment

Fig. 14 A jamming equipment

Much of electronic warfare is shrouded in secrecy which creates an air of mystery
and confusion in the minds of many in the army not immediately concerned in it.
On the other hand, naval and air forces have, since the 1939 - 45 war considered
EW as an everyday part of warfare. Radar capabilities and jamming, missile

guidance jamming and communications intercept are routine to them. Warsaw Pact armies have developed the concept of co-ordinating EW into just another form of gathering intelligence and improving their offensive capability. NATO was not so quick off the mark, but in more recent years an awareness of the potential of EW has increased in NATO armies.

In this brief review only the common sense and organisation of EW and an explanation of some of the specialist terms will be covered, but for those interested more detail is contained in Volumes 6 and 8 of this series.

Logic and Language of EW

The basic logic of EW is first of all to find, and find out all about the enemy's equipment using electronic devices: the specialist term for this is Electronic Support Measures (ESM). Secondly, and based upon the information gained by ESM, the next stage is to upset the enemy's electronic equipment by jamming or deception: this is called Electronic Counter Measures (ECM). Thirdly, the enemy must be prevented from employing ECM against us, so we employ care and discipline, combined with both physical and electronic deception to protect our communications, our surveillance and target acquisition equipment and our GW guidance systems; this is called Electronic Counter Counter Measures (ECCM).

Command and Control of EW

ESM and ECM are the province of specialist units. They deploy along the FEBA with equipment to detect and analyse electronic signals being emitted by the enemy. A detection equipment is shown in Fig. 13. If considered necessary and it is tactically expedient then jammers, which are also deployed along the FEBA, are brought into operation. A photograph of a jamming equipment is in Fig. 14.

When the ESM intelligence on the enemy has been collected, the decision on the use of ECM obviously lies with the tactical commander, relating it to his overall tactical plan. It may be that the timing for jamming some target, such as an enemy headquarters, may be critical to a commander's plan. It may be, too, that the delivery of small expendable jammers, say on an enemy's counter-battery position, may require co-ordination with artillery commanders. To ensure that commanders are advised and their orders put into effect, EW staff are to be found at formation headquarters. They vary from Electronic Warfare Liaison Officers (EWLO) at lower headquarters to Electronic Warfare Control Centres (EWCC) at higher levels.

Command and Control ECCM

Surveillance devices, target acquisition devices and GW ECCM are mentioned in Chapters 7 and 8. The ECCM measures which can protect our own headquarters and communication systems depend on some understanding of how an enemy can detect and jam our communications. In fact his detection system consists of two or more sensitive receivers with antennas which turn; they are similar to that shown in Fig. 13. Two of them can, by re-section, fix the location of a transmitter as demonstrated in Fig. 15.

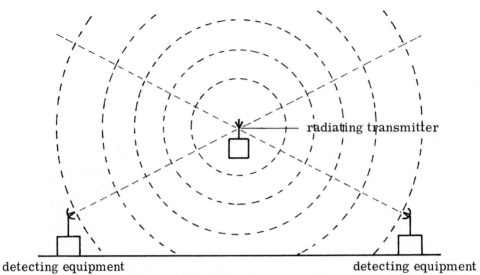

radiating transmitter

detecting equipment   detecting equipment
Fig. 15   Location of a transmitter

From this simple illustration we can work out that there are a few measures possible to prevent detection by detecting equipment which is, after all, most often
further away than the friendly stations for whom the transmission is intended.
One measure to be taken is to design sets with no more range than they require
and if they are fitted with a high power boost capability to increase range when
necessary the operator should only use it when it is essential. Fortunately those
troops nearest the FEBA do not normally need much range and are often very
mobile which makes it difficult for enemy ECM to fix their position. Another well
tried measure is to change frequency as often as is feasible. Technology now
allows this frequency hopping to be carried out automatically at a very fast rate
and future radios may well incorporate such a facility. Of course the best method
is not to transmit at all if it is avoidable: radio silence is a very effective ECCM.
If permanent silence is not possible then transmitting time should be cut down to a
minimum so making it difficult for an enemy intercept which is tuning frequencies
and trying to find the direction of a signal to achieve a fix. Again it is now possible to design a system of recording a message, whether voice, code or in data
form and then transmit that message in a burst at a greatly speeded up rate: it is
called 'burst transmission' and cuts down the time during which the enemy intercept stations can make a fix.

Careful siting of radios or radio relay terminals is very important. A radio
relay link should not be sited, if possible, so that it is in line with the enemy; this
would avoid the possibility of the signal over-spilling into his territory. If possible high ground, which would effectively screen the UHF and SHF frequencies of
modern radio relay links, should be kept between the terminals and the enemy.
In addition the narrower the beam of a signal the more difficult it is for enemy
intercept to pick up.

If, however, these precautions are ineffective and the enemy is able to beam in a jammer on to a station then an answer is to change or hop to another frequency. Such a procedure must be part of well understood Standing Operating Procedures (SOPs).   Of course, if that station is also within range of enemy artillery or not well protected by air defence then it would be wise to move it very smartly.

Summary

Technical advances are improving ESM, ECM and ECCM and some of these have been outlined. It remains as always, that good radio discipline, good training and good siting can do much to ensure that the enemy ECM is unable to be effect- ive.   The newer element of EW is that it is now regarded as yet another offensive or defensive system in a commander's armoury to be used as part of his integ- rated tactical plan.

Annex to Chapter 6

	FREQUENCY MHz	TRANSMISSION	RANGE km	miles
MANPACKS				
PRC-350	36-57	Voice (FM)	5	3
PRC-351	30-76	Voice (FM) Digital data*	8	5
PRC-352	30-76	Voice (FM) Digital data*	16	10
PRC-320	2-29.9999	Voice Morse	50 300	30 200 (sky)
VEHICLE				
VRC-353	30-75.975	Voice (FM) Facsimile* Telegraph* Digital data*	30	20
VRC-321	1.5-29.9999	Voice (AM) Morse RTT FSK	50 300+	30 200+ (Sky)
VRC-322	1.5-29.9999	Voice (AM) Morse RTT FSK	80 300+	50 200+ (Sky)

Note the frequency overlap of both the VHF and HF sets.   This allows interoperability when it is required.

---

* Require separate applique units

SELF TEST QUESTIONS

Question 1   What is a main reason, apart from cost and complexity, for not
              using television as a military communication system?

              Answer ....
              ....

Question 2   What are the advantages and disadvantages of a HF radio net
              compared with a VHF radio net?

              a Advantages ....
                             ....
                             ....

              b Disadvantages ....
                             ....
                             ....
                             ....
                             ....
                             ....
                             ....
                             ....

Question 3   What are the advantages of developing a family of net radio sets
              rather than adopting a variety of individually developed sets?

              Answer ....
                      ....
                      ....
                      ....
                      ....
                      ....

Question 4   Why is there a requirement for commercial radio for military use?

Answer ....

....

....

....

Question 5   What other facilities apart from open voice communications are available in a modern trunk communication system?

Answer ....

....

....

....

Question 6   Why is an area communication system less vulnerable than a chain of command communication system?

Answer ....

....

....

Question 7   What are the advantages to be gained from a computer to aid the command and control functions of a headquarters?

Answer ....

....

....

....

....

....

Question 8   Define in general terms:

a Electronic Support Measures (ESM):

....

....

b Electronic Counter Measures (ECM):

....

....

c Electronic Counter Counter Measures (ECCM):

....

....

Question 9   What equipments are used to provide ESM and ECM?

Answer ....

....

Question 10   What ECCM measures can be taken to prevent an enemy using his ECM capability?

Answer ....

....

....

....

....

....

....

ANSWERS ON PAGE   181

7

Surveillance and Target Acquisition

AN ARMY'S REQUIREMENT

An army's ability to react effectively to the opposing forces depends much on its ability to discover their dispositions and concentrations. Scouts and informers have always played a large part in the outcome of battles. If Napoleon, Blucher and Wellington had known the details of each others' dispositions in those critical few days before Waterloo, it is doubtful that the battle, although inevitable, would have been fought where it was and the outcome might have been different.

In a modern land battle, quick reaction to an enemy's concentrations of mechanised forces is decisive. Considerable information of large concentrations before hostilities can be gained from satellites, but weather conditions may often prevent detailed observation and satellites may well be destroyed at the onset of hostilities. In such a situation surveillance from aircraft is the next line of approach, but again this very much depends on achieving air superiority and the suppression of the enemy air defence carpet: as was discovered in the Yom Kippur war this is not always very easy. Nevertheless, surveillance to provide the intelligence on which commanders can base their plans and to enable targets to be acquired for weapon systems is an essential part of any army's capability and must be pursued despite difficulties and losses.

The majority of the immediate surveillance will be carried out by ground forces and a major problem is how to improve on line of sight from a ground observer. Armies have always tried to improve on this ability as the brave artillery observation officers in their balloons during the 1914 - 18 war testified. Possibly the main limiting factor on the effective use of modern artillery is the ability to find the target in order to use the range available. Before looking at methods of solving this problem, however, it is important to look at how an army can improve its line of sight performance beyond that of the eye-ball enhanced by binoculars.

First of all, it is useful to be clear about what is required. Basically we want to:

<blockquote>
Detect   -   'Something is there'
Recognise   -   'It is a tank/body of men'
</blockquote>

Identify   -   'It is a T72 tank/they are enemy soldiers
Locate   -   'Grid reference ...'

RADAR

Radio Detection and Ranging (RADAR) is good for detecting targets and is able to
a limited extent to recognise some. It has a long range, compared with other
surveillance systems, because it uses comparatively long waves. In this respect
it can be compared to radio communications, as described in Chapter 6: the HF
signals using long waves have a much greater range than VHF or UHF signals
using shorter waves.

Surveillance devices using long waves, in addition to their range advantage, can
also penetrate through smoke, mist and rain better than those using shorter wave
techniques.

A brief look at how a radar system works will help in assessing its advantages
and disadvantages.

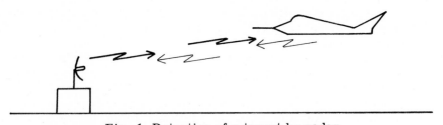

Fig. 1 Detection of a target by radar

It works very like a torchlight beam in which the bulb acts as a source of light and
the reflector narrows the light into a beam. When the light illuminates an object
the light is reflected back to the observer holding the torchlight. In a radar an
antenna replaces the bulb: it is fed with, and radiates, radio waves. They are
narrowed into a beam by a dish or some other form of reflecting device and then
the radio waves illuminate an object and are reflected back to a receiver. Radar
has two advantages over light and indeed over other surveillance methods: it can
measure the distance to the target it illuminates and it can measure its speed.
Other surveillance systems need the addition of a Laser Range Finder (LRF) to
measure distance and they can not, as yet, measure speed.

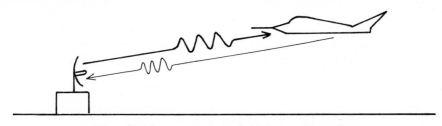

Fig. 2 Measurement of distance by radar

It measures distance by sending out pulses of waves. It is known that radar waves travel at the speed of light. So if the time is measured from the moment a pulse leaves the radar to the time when the reflected pulse arrives back, then a simple calculation can determine the distance of the target. For example: the speed of light is 300,000,000 m/sec. If the time from the pulse's departure to its return is $\dfrac{1}{30,000}$ sec then the pulse will have travelled a total of $\dfrac{300,000,000 \text{ m/sec}}{30,000 \text{ sec}} =$ 10,000 m or 10 km. The distance to the target is half that distance, because the pulse has travelled there and back, so it is 5 km.

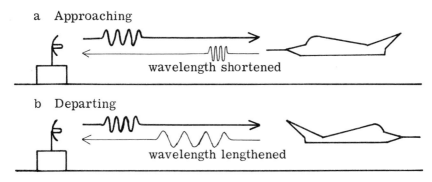

a Approaching

wavelength shortened

b Departing

wavelength lengthened

Fig. 3 Measurement of speed by radar

Speed is measured by using the doppler shift effect. It works because the wavelength returning is changed from that emitted, by the direction and speed of the target. An approaching target results in a shorter wavelength: the faster the target is approaching, the shorter the returning wavelength becomes. A similar effect is created by a target travelling away from the radar: in this case, though, the returning wavelength is increased.

So far only simple targets like aircraft with a clear sky behind have been considered; it is much more difficult when the target is on the ground with many other objects cluttering the background. A radar looking for a target in such a scene has the same difficulty in finding it as a person has trying to find someone they know in a crowded street. The background effect is known as ground clutter. The difficulty is increased because a long wave device is less able to discriminate between one object, or target, than is a shorter wave device. A shorter wave radar becomes necessary for ground target location but, of course, this results in a reduction of range and the ability to penetrate rain, mist and smoke; so there is a balance to be struck.

One advantage in shortening the range of a radar to its minimum is to reduce its chance of being detected by enemy Electronic Counter Measures (ECM) devices. A radar is easy to detect because it acts, as we have seen, like a beam of light. A torch can be seen at a much greater distance than it can see an object, because it relies on relatively weak reflected light to do so. A radar is similar. Once detected the radar, whether it is being used for surveillance only or is a target acquisition radar for a GW, can be jammed easily; this is analagous to a person with a torch being blinded by one which is shone back at him. Any active system suffers from this disadvantage. Active infra-red surveillance devices and sights were superseded because they could be easily detected, but passive infra-red, or

thermal imaging devices as they are more descriptively named, are not easy to
detect. Any detected device can be subject to jamming or deception by a false
signal or destruction.

THERMAL IMAGING

Thermal imaging systems act like television systems. In a television camera the
object of interest is focussed on to a light sensitive plate which translates the
picture into electronic signals. These are transmitted to a television receiver,
by microwave communication links or cable, where they are reconstructed into a
visual picture on a Cathode Ray Tube (CRT), or in other words on the television
screen. In a thermal imaging system the only difference is that instead of a light
sensitive plate there is a pattern of heat sensors which can 'see' or sense small
differences in temperature, so in effect they are looking at a heat picture. From
then on the system is the same as a normal television system.

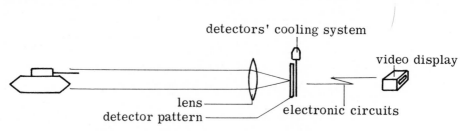

Fig. 4 Outline of thermal imaging system

In front of the detector pattern must be a lens to focus the heat from the target on
to the pattern. The lens material can not be glass because it does not let through
the thermal radiation; instead it is normally an expensive Germanium lens, which
does. Yet another complication is caused by the need to cool the detectors: they
must be cooled by liquid nitrogen or a mini cooling engine to -196°C. This adds
cost and complication to thermal imaging devices; but for the immediate future,
for an effective imaging system, it is necessary.

Thermal imagers can be used very effectively as pure surveillance devices and
although they are not so good at it as radar, they are able to see through rain,
mist, smoke and the fog of battle to a considerable extent and are very useful out
to four or five kilometres. In addition the thermal imaging technique has two
great advantages over radar. First it can produce a good enough image to recognise and identify targets: a tank looks like a tank and a man looks like a man as
can be seen in Fig. 5. The second advantage is that a thermal imaging device can
be used as a sight; what is more its range matches those of tank guns and ATGW
very well. Tanks, MICVs and ATGW in the future will have thermal imaging
sights and some are currently about to come into service.

Electronic warfare can intrude into the thermal imaging scene also. It is not
very difficult to see that thermal decoys could be made to confuse imagers: indeed
a very hot object would 'blind' a device in a similar way to a very bright light
being shone at a pair of binoculars or a strong radar beam being directed at a
radar receiver.

Fig. 5 Thermal images of men and a tank

IMAGE INTENSIFICATION

Equally passive in their use, and so not easy to detect, are image intensifiers. The fundamental idea of an image intensifier is to take a telescope and put in it an image intensification tube which amplifies the light level often by 40,000 times or more. Fig. 6 shows the principle.

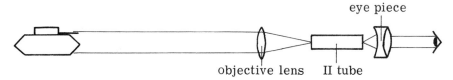

eye piece

objective lens   II tube

Fig. 6 Outline of an image intensification sight

The front, or objective lens, focusses the target on to the front of the image intensification tube. The light amplification takes place and the brightened image appears on the rear face of the tube. All that is then required is an eye-piece to look at it.

Fig. 7 Image intensification sight on a rifle

The soldier shown with an Individual Weapon Sight (IWS) in Fig. 7, on a clear star-lit night with no moon, could probably pick out a man at three or four hundred metres. Of course, normal camouflage rules apply as in daylight, so a well cam-ouflaged target remains a well camouflaged target even at night.

The effective range of an image intensifier depends very much on the size of the front or objective lens put in front of the tube. A large lens collects much more light from a target than a small lens. For this reason a proper surveillance device such as 'Twiggy', shown in Fig. 8, is much larger than a small arms sight even though it employs a similar tube to the IWS.

On a clear starlit night its effective range would be two or three times that of the IWS. The IWS on the other hand is comparatively large for a rifle, LMG or GPMG: at approximately 3 kg it nearly doubles the weight of a modern rifle. Consequently a smaller sight, based on a more powerful single stage intensification tube, is coming into service.

An image intensifier can see white lights at great distances even if they are very low. A side advantage is that they can also detect active infra-red searchlights, weapon sights or headlights: they see them as white light. There is little doubt that this ability could be of considerable use against an enemy using active IR. It is also a good reason for not using active IR ourselves. Most modern AFVs are now being fitted with image intensifier drivers' sights to eradicate the danger inherent in the use of active IR headlights.

Fig. 8 Twiggy image intensification surveillance device

Compared with radar or thermal imaging, image intensification devices have a much shorter range and cannot see through rain or smoke. Consequently they are not so useful as sights for weapons with long ranges and are not such good surveillance devices as thermal imagers. Conversely for short ranges, they are smaller, handier and cheaper than other systems: so they are useful on small weapons, on patrols and are on a more generous scale of issue than can be afforded for thermal imagers. It can be foreseen that thermal imaging may well replace image intensifiers as surveillance devices in the not too distant future, but it is difficult to imagine a thermal imaging sight on small arms, or in the hands of a patrol commander, for some time yet.

LASERS

Lasers are not surveillance devices in their own right. They are able to enhance the capability of an image intensifier by providing a narrow beam of light to illum- inate the target, but such devices are somewhat complicated and expensive. Their two great uses, to date, are range finding and target marking; it has also been demonstrated that lasers can be used for communication links but as yet no military systems have been produced. When they do they will probably be connected to fibre optic cables which are much lighter than conventional cables.

As a range finder, a laser works in a similar way to radar. A pulse is sent out and the time to its return measured. Using this technique lasers can measure a range to an accuracy within 5 m. It is therefore of great use to FOOs, but per- haps its greatest impact has been its enhancement of tank guns effectiveness. The ability to determine a target's range accurately has improved the ability of a high velocity APDS or APFSDS round to obtain a first hit, but much more it has dram- atically improved the overall hit probability of the lower velocity HESH and HEAT rounds, for which range estimation is far more critical. It is now, in theory, pos- sible for a tank gun to fire HESH and HEAT to an effective range of six thousand metres or more, but the practical acquisition of the target at such ranges in Central Europe may pose some problems.

The use of the 'Smart' bomb first announced the potential of laser designation or target marking. If a laser can be aimed at a target then a bomb, missile or shell with a sensor in its nose can detect the reflections of the laser from the target and home in on it. Such a method could be used to direct ATGW or even shells/ missiles launched indirectly by artillery. A system for designating indirectly fired projectiles is shown diagrammatically in Fig. 9. The projectile is called a Cannon Launched Guided Projectile (CLGP).

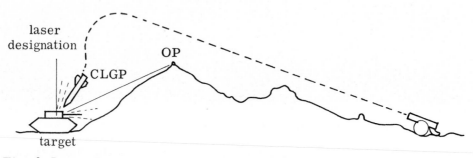

Fig. 9 Laser designation for cannon launched guided projectile (CLGP)

The system is limited by the range at which an OP can acquire his target. It would be much less limited if the designation could be carried out from the air with consequently longer acquisition ranges: it could certainly be achieved from heli- copters but they would be required to expose themselves for considerable lengths of time. As an alternative it has been proposed that the designation could be carried out from unmanned Remotely Piloted Vehicles (RPVs).

REMOTELY PILOTED VEHICLES

RPVs can provide a commander with the ability to improve on the limited line of sight surveillance possible from the ground. So far, RPVs are not highly developed but most advanced nations are putting effort into them.

In the British Army the current system for unmanned aerial reconnaissance is to use a drone: it is named 'Midge'. It is launched from behind the FEBA and follows a pre-planned flight path, during which it takes films. On its return to base, the film is recovered and developed. Only then, some time after the mission, is the information available to the staff. It would be a much more useful device if the information could be immediate, or 'real-time' in current jargon and if the flight path could be controlled and monitored so that targets and information could be found whilst the vehicle was in the air.

A well controlled RPV could be used more for a greater variety of tasks than photography. It could be extended in its scope as illustrated in Fig. 10.

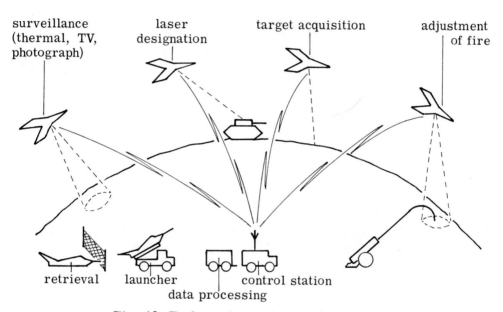

Fig. 10 Tasks and organisation for RPVs

A television and thermal imaging capability is required for surveillance, target detection and identification and then fire adjustment. It is also difficult to envisage that a laser target designator could be used without the assistance of a television or thermal imager to provide the necessary reference picture.

It quickly becomes apparent that if the advantages to be derived from the use of RPVs are to be used well, a considerable control and communication organisation is necessary. If a commander thought that the information gleaned from RPVs was of sufficient importance he could have a receiver, probably a Visual Display Unit (VDU), with his intelligence staff, so it could be acted upon quickly.

Fig. 11   Fixed wing RPV

The use of television channels would take up a considerable bandwidth in the
communications band and more communication links would be required to guide
the RPV and point the surveillance device or laser.   ECM would almost certainly
be used against RPVs by an enemy, so ECCM should be built in.   The cost and
complication of the whole system would necessarily become considerable, but it
would provide a vitally needed facility.

The RPV itself can be one of three basic forms, fixed wing, rotary wing and
tethered.   The fixed wing, similar to the RPV shown in Fig. 11 can fly forward
well and make tight circles with its surveillance system and laser locked on.   It
uses much less fuel than a rotary wing RPV which cannot move so quickly: conversely a rotary wing craft is able to hover and thus provide a steady constant
picture of a target or area of intelligence interest.   The tethered RPV is normally
a rotary wing device.   Because it is tethered it can only be used from behind the
FEBA and so its only advantage is height.   On the other hand it can be small,
because the fuel can be fed up the tethering cable.   Its very smallness makes it
difficult to detect.   A Canadian prototype is shown in Fig. 12.

Detection of the RPV by visual means, noise, radar and thermal devices must all
be minimised.   To some extent all are immediately made difficult if the RPV can

Fig. 12 Rotary Wing RPV

be small and thus require only a low powered engine which would be quieter and give off less heat than a larger engine. In practice if the RPV can be kept below a length of 2 m with slender wings and body, then its detection is not easy: some RPVs under development are this small. If it is possible within such small dimensions to design an equipment which will reach out to a distance of sixty or seventy kilometres beyond the FEBA; a commander would then have time to react to detected enemy movements and find targets for his long range artillery weapons such as FFR. It appears that RPVs with such a range will be possible and the rapid advance of micro electronic technology will assist greatly in the development of detection devices to fit into them.

UNATTENDED GROUND SENSORS (UGS)

The only other way a commander can obtain information from over the horizon, except by sending out a patrol, is by employing Unattended Ground Sensors (UGS) and again the use of 'micro-chip' technology will do much to advance their use. The devices themselves are normally seismic, thermal, magnetic or acoustic sensors of which the first two have been most widely used to date.

A seismic device is based on a geophone which can detect very small tremors in the ground, such as a footfall or the movement of a vehicle. The problem is to ensure that it 'reports' only those tremors of military significance. This is where 'micro-chips' come into their own. It is possible to construct electronic circuitry which will filter out all tremors but those of the particular patterns, such as those produced by a tank, in which the UGS controller is interested. When such a pattern occurs the UGS can be programmed to send a radio signal.

It now takes only a little ingenuity to see that UGS placed at critical points along routes or in defiles can build up a total pattern of enemy movement which can be used for intelligence or target acquisition purposes.

The same principles can apply whatever type of sensor is used. They must be selective in what they report and they must be placed in critical positions. Their emplacement may pose problems, but the means open are delivery by artillery, aircraft or RPV or they could be left behind during a withdrawal.

SUMMARY

The rapid advancement in electronic miniaturisation will enable a greater use of sensors for surveillance and target acquisition purposes. It will permit smaller, more rugged equipment and it will result in more discriminatory devices which will report or display only the relevant information. The omens are that the next decade will see the practical translation into military equipment of the devices which have been developed during the past decade.

SELF TEST QUESTIONS

Question 1   What are the four main requirements from a surveillance system?

Answer ....

....

....

....

Question 2   What advantages and disadvantages has radar compared with other surveillance systems?

Advantages ....

....

....

....

....

Disadvantages ....

....

....

Question 3   If the time taken for a radar pulse to travel to a target and return is $\frac{1}{15,000}$ sec, what is the range to the target?

Answer ....

....

....

....

....

....

Question 4   What are the advantages to be gained from the use of thermal imaging systems?

Answer ....

....

....

....

Question 5   What is the basic principle of the operation of an image
              intensification device?

Answer ....

....

....

Question 6   What are the advantages and disadvantages of an image intensifier
              compared with other surveillance systems?

Advantages ....

....

....

....

....

Disadvantages ....

....

Question 7   What are the two main military roles currently performed by a
              laser device?

Answer ....

....

Question 8   What future military use do you envisage for lasers?

Answer ....

Question 9   What is the main surveillance advantage to be gained from the
              use of RPVs?

Answer ....

....

Question 10 What are the main types of sensors used by UGS?

Answer ....

....

....

....

ANSWERS ON PAGE 182

8

Guided Weapons
(Including Light Anti-Armour Weapons)

THE ROLES OF GUIDED WEAPONS

The essential difference between a guided weapon and any other form of projectile, whether it be a rocket or a shell, is that it continues to be guided on to its target after launch. In other systems the accuracy is achieved by the correct alignment of the projectile before it is launched or fired.

Guns have the advantage that once they have been bought, the ammunition is much cheaper than a rocket or guided weapon. The ammunition is also smaller than a rocket or guided weapon, so a gun system pays less of a logistic penalty.

On the other hand guided weapons have, over the past twenty-five years, enabled surface to surface indirect fire systems to increase their ranges many times over; they have become by far the major component of air defence systems; they have given infantry the ability to destroy Main Battle Tanks (MBTs); they have enabled the engagement of MBTs at greater ranges than anti-tank guns.

This chapter covers guided weapons used in army systems and gives an insight into their operation.

Components of a Guided Weapon

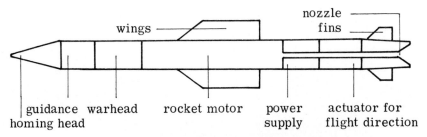

Fig. 1 Components of a guided weapon

155

Fig. 1 gives a diagrammatic picture of a guided weapon's components. Not all guided weapons have all the components shown, nor are they necessarily in the same configuration. By no means do all weapons have homing heads, or wings as well as fins. Control is normally achieved by fin movement or nozzle movement.

The essential parts of a guided weapon are a warhead to do the damage, a guidance system to guide the weapon to its target, an actuator to vary the flight by moving the fins or nozzle, a power supply for the guidance package and to drive the actuator, a motor and at least one pair of wings or fins, except for guided shells. The sizes and the complexity of the components will vary with their role, the lethality required and the range demanded. Perhaps the simplest and certainly the smallest are the Anti-Tank Guided Weapons (ATGWs).

ANTI-TANK WEAPONS

Gun Limitations

A direct fire anti-tank gun has two limitations: it is not easily portable and it begins to lose accuracy over approximately 2,000 m. A quick study of British anti-tank guns shows that during the 1939 - 45 war, as tanks became better armoured, so the guns starting with the relatively light and mobile two pounder increased in size to a six pounder and then a seventeen pounder, which weighed nearly three tons and was in service at the end of the war. Even so it was not man enough for the task and a thirty-two pounder weighing approximately six tons was built but never brought into service, though it can be seen as an ornament outside the British Army's School of Infantry Support Weapons Wing. Such cumbersome guns could not be moved around or concealed easily in forward positions.

Fig. 2 Fire Support Combat Vehicle

Some anti-tank guns were made more mobile by putting them on tracked chassis and the tank destroyer was born. They have a part to play and still exist: the West German Jagdpanzer is an example and even more up to date is the Fire Support Combat Vehicle, which is a German concept based on a United States M 113 chassis. Unfortunately they are costly and few countries can afford to buy and maintain both tank destroyers and tanks, so they concentrate on the more versatile tank which can double up as a tank destroyer.

The great advantage of an anti-tank gun is that it can fire all three forms of anti-armour projectile, kinetic energy, HESH and HEAT, but its range is inherently limited by the need for accurate range estimation, errors in laying the gun, lack of ammunition consistency, effects of wind drift and the need to estimate accurately the target's crossing speed.

By using recoilless guns such as the American 106 mm and the British Wombat 120 mm, it has been possible to reduce the weight of guns drastically, but unfortunately their effective range is reduced also; nor are they sufficiently light to permit easy manoeuvring in forward positions.

Light Unguided Anti-tank Weapons

Whilst guns were gaining weight, another line of approach which exploited the inherent lightness of the HEAT warhead was being followed; it was a series of shoulder launched anti-tank weapons which we now know generically as Light Anti-tank Weapons (LAWs)

Fig. 3 Carl Gustav FV 550

There are two main types of launcher and the first is based on the rocket principle. The American Bazooka was perhaps the most famous and it was the fore-
runner of the 3. 5 Rocket Launcher. The launcher needs to be of a reasonable
length to allow the rocket to gain a reasonable speed before it exits: it must be all
burnt before it exits so that the burning rocket motor's efflux does not damage the
firer's face. Because the rocket does not have a high launching speed, it has a
poor effective range; it is probably confined to less than 200 m. On the other hand
it is light and, as evinced by the very light (2. 2 kg) M 72, American 66 mm
rocket launcher, the tube can be disposable.

The Swedish firm Carl Gustav have proved that greater ranges can be gained by
using a recoilless system. The penalty is a heavier launcher, because it must
withstand a sudden high pressure as it fires. The FV 550 system weighs 15 kg
without the 3. 2 kg shell and 3. 4 kg sight, but it can achieve effective ranges of
more than 700 m with the aid of its quite complicated sight.

The Russian RPG 7 is a very interesting adaptation of the rocket system which
allows both a reasonable sized warhead and small launcher. It does this by
having a small charge which throws it clear of the firer and its launcher before
the main rocket motor ignites and drives it to its target. The projectile fits into
the launcher like a spigot which enables a relatively large warhead with a thin
launcher. Fig. 4 shows the configuration. The main problem, however, of any
rocket which ignites in flight is accuracy, because it may give the initial boost
when the projectile is wobbling, as it does.

Fig. 4 Russian RPG 7

Another interesting adaptation, this time of the recoilless system, is the French
Strim. It consists of a 5. 4 kg launcher on to which fits the 3. 8 kg projectile
package in its own tube. The initial thrust and pressure is taken by the projectile's package which is discarded: the launcher takes only a little of the thrust and
is designed to stand one hundred launchings or more. Such a system manages to
amalgamate both lightness with the retention of the tube. Inherent in this method
is the advantage of retaining a good sighting system. A throwaway tube can only
have a cheap sight or a strap on sight with its attendant alignment difficulties.

Fig. 5 French Strim

The problem which faces a designer is to produce a weapon, with a sufficiently large warhead to penetrate a MBT's armour, and a powerful enough rocket motor to propel it to a satisfactory distance. He must also keep it light enough to be operated by one man and safe enough to be fired from the shoulder without damaging the firer.

These limitations, over the past four decades have kept the hollow charge warheads down to a diameter of 80 - 90 mm and, as is explained in Chapter 3, armour penetration is closely allied to this diameter. The Carl Gustav FV 550 and Strim need two men to carry and operate them and even so they will find it difficult to penetrate the front of the latest MBTs, especially with the advent of compound armours which degrade the effect of hollow charge warheads by a considerable amount.

In simple terms the choice for a new LAW comes down to a large warhead which can penetrate the frontal armour of a tank or a small warhead which can penetrate the side only. A large warhead will result in a large weapon, and probably a two man team, or a short range weapon operated by one man, or a balance of the two. A small warhead permits a longer range or a lighter weapon or, again, a balance of these two. It is the availability of manpower and the tactical doctrine which will decide which concept the soldier will favour.

Research also continues into making an effective shoulder launch anti-tank weapon which can be fired from a normal sized room in a building: at present the backblast prevents it. Such a capability is more than desirable for urban warfare conditions. As yet the problem has not been fully solved but an attempt to do so has been made with a German Armbrust shoulder launched weapon: unfortunately the solution, in which the backblast is absorbed by material packed in the rear of the launcher, entails considerable increase in weight; this increase has so far prevented the development of a weapon which can be effective against head-on MBTs but yet light enough to be fired from the shoulder from inside a normal sized room.

In a mechanised war environment, infantrymen must be prepared and armed to

stand up to and destroy armoured vehicles. At present the unguided lightweight
shoulder launched weapons cannot take on the front of the latest MBTs protected
by compound armour; but they are effective when used in defilade. If a warhead
could be developed to defeat the frontal armour of a MBT, the weapon would still
be limited in range both by sighting inaccuracies and the lack or power which
could safely be packed into the propellant of a shoulder launched weapon. They
would, however, be effective against the side of MBTs and even more so against
APCs and MICVs: this would make a mechanised infantry attack, in which they
drove on to the objective, a very hazardous operation.

LAWs are complementary to ATGW which have a limited minimum range, but are
able to reach out to greater ranges - more than an anti-tank gun. This capability
is not gained without penalties: they are normally crew served weapons, taking
two or three men to man them; they are more complicated, which involves more
training to man them; finally they are much more costly.

Anti-tank Guided Weapons

Fig. 6 The Milan ATGW

By the end of the 1939 - 45 war the Germans had reached the drawing board stage
in the development of their XH7 ATGW which was intended to have a range of
1,000 m. Its influence can be seen in the first SS 10 French ATGW introduced in
1955 and the Russian Snapper which was first seen in 1958.

Earlier in this chapter it was noted that the two main advantages which ATGW enjoy over anti-tank guns are lightweight and range. As would be expected however the longer the range the heavier the missile, because it requires a larger motor. The propellant or propulsion unit has two main functions: it must boost the missile to its flying speed and then sustain it at that speed. Most missiles have two motors, one for boosting and one for sustaining: the speed of the missile depends upon the size of the boost motor and its range upon the size of the sustainer motor.

Once launched the missile operator guides the missile on to the target. Virtually all ATGW use a Command to Line of Sight (CLOS) guidance. This means that the missile is flown along the line of sight from the tracker to the target, being commanded or guided back on to it when it wanders off line. The first generation of equipments such as the Russian Sagger, the British Vigilant and the French SS 11 all use Manual Command to Line of Sight (MCLOS): see Fig. 7.

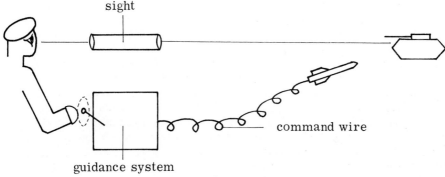

sight

command wire

guidance system

Fig. 7 Elements of MCLOS guidance

In such systems, the human operator, after launching the missile, has two functions to perform: he tracks the target and guides the missile on to the line of sight through a wire payed out from the missile.

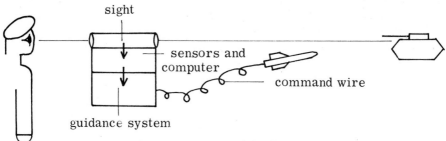

sight

sensors and computer

command wire

guidance system

Fig. 8 Elements of SACLOS guidance

Second generation missiles make the task of the human operator much more simple by including a Semi-automatic Command to Line of Sight (SACLOS) system. In such systems, as can be seen from Fig. 8, the operator has only to track the target by keeping the sight aligned on it. The missile is commanded on to the line of sight by sensors in the launcher system which sense when the missile moves away from the line: a computer then calculates the signal to be transmitted to the missile to steer it back on to the line.

It is probably relevant, at this stage to look at some of the problems which face the firer and the solutions to them. SACLOS is the first help he can be given but, because the launcher system is asked to perform an extra task, to command the flight of the missile, it is more expensive. Whether the missile is first (MCLOS), or second (SACLOS), generation, the concentration required from the operator during the whole flight of the missile is an important consideration, especially when the operator is subjected to battlefield conditions of stress and distraction. Designers can help by cutting down the times of flight with a faster flying missile. This has already happened to some extent: whereas a German Mamba took approximately 17.5 sec to cover 3,000 m, the American Tow takes 15 sec. The penalty to pay for these higher speeds is more propellant to provide more boost and so the weight goes up.

The ideal missile from the operator's point of view would be a fire and forget system and this is the definition of a third generation ATGW. A fully autonamous ATGW would be a missile with a passive homing system. The operator would launch the missile towards the target; as the gap between them narrowed, a homing device in the nose of the missile would lock on to the target and steer on to it. Unfortunately locking on to a target on the ground, which may be amongst other moving vehicles or even just trees and buildings, is not nearly so easy as locking on to an aeroplane in a clear sky or a ship on the comparatively flat surface of the sea. The most likely ATGW homing system would be heat seeking and so subject to being decoyed by false heat sources. A radar homing system would have difficulty in recognising the target amongst the background clutter.

An easier solution would be a semi-active homing device which worked in conjunction with a laser designator. This would enable the missile to be launched from behind cover or from a helicopter which can then take cover, and the target would be illuminated by an operator, with a laser, from a line of sight position.

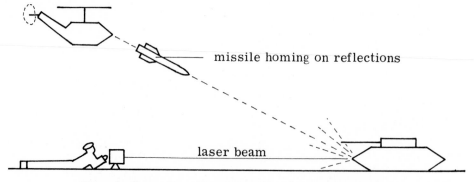

missile homing on reflections

laser beam

Fig. 9 Operation of semi-active homing system

It is for conjecture whether this semi-active system has sufficient advantages over a SACLOS system to be worth while. It achieves separation and perhaps more importantly allows a fast re-engagement of new targets by the launcher operators who have 'forgotten' the launched missile. So there is a consequent increase in the rate of fire. The first disadvantage is cost: it would be several times more costly than the SACLOS system, as would all homing systems. The second is that a highly reliable communications link would be required between the launching team and the laser designator operator.

If weight is not such a pressing problem and the missile need not be crew portable, then it can be made with a larger warhead and a larger propulsion unit to give it greater speed. To date, the British Swingfire has the largest warhead at 7 kg followed by the French/German Hot missile. They are very suitable for long ranges out to 4,000 m and for firing from vehicles. The British Army fits Swingfire on its FV 438 and Striker vehicles.

The longer range missiles are also suitable for fitting to helicopters, an idea first pioneered by the French in Algeria for guiding missiles into caves. Now they and the West Germans fit the SACLOS Hot missile to their helicopters, the Americans and the British fit Tow, another SACLOS missile, whilst the Russians have now also fitted their SACLOS Swatter and Spiral.

Anti-tank Defence System

ATGW combined with anti-tank guns, tank guns and shoulder launched LAW give a comprehensive anti-tank defence. Attrition of enemy armour can begin at ranges of 4,000 m by long range ATGW. At 3,000 m tank and anti-tank guns can join in. At 2,000 m crew portable ATGW, manned by infantry, become effective.

Fig. 10 Striker vehicle firing Swingfire

At 1,000 m missiles which can be operated by one man, like the American Dragon, come into play. At 500 m LAWs begin to be effective and tend to take over from ATGW, which below 200 m are difficult to control with accuracy.

ATGW have limited use in built up areas. At very short ranges, say up to 40 or 50 m, they could be launched directly at tanks, unguided. From 50 - 200 m they are unlikely to be of use and there are very few shoots over 200 m in towns. LAWs will be the main effective anti-tank weapons and the conditions will be very suitable for defilade fire from the side or overhead. A major limitation, however, is the inability of ATGW and LAW to fire from buildings with normal sized rooms, without causing injury to the firer.

SURFACE TO SURFACE GUIDED WEAPONS (SSGW)

Although the literal meaning of Surface to Surface Guided Weapons (SSGW) includes ATGW, in normal military usage it is confined to indirect fire weapons. SSGW take over from Free Flight Rockets (FFR) when the range demands an accuracy, which can only be gained by a guidance system more refined than pointing the rocket in the correct direction at the correct angle and calculating when to cut off the fuel. FFRs are dealt with in Chapter 2.

SSGW can be classified in many ways but in this chapter only a division between strategic and tactical missiles will be made. The cut off for tactical weapons we will take as 2,000 km.

Warheads

Very expensive guided weapons, the accuracy of which is unlikely to be calculated in less than hundreds of metres, are only occasionally likely to be used with conventional warheads. They are almost certain to have nuclear warheads and these vary from sub-kiloton devices, as in the case of the American Lance which has a range of 20 km, to warheads which have a 50 MT capability as in the case of the Russian SS 18. It is explained in Chapter 4 that the larger nuclear warheads do not give a correspondingly larger effect: there is a law of diminishing returns. Now the tendency is to use multiple warheads with smaller yields. For example the SS 18 in its second version, has up to eight Multiple Independently Targetted Re-entry Vehicles (MIRVs) each with a yield of approximately 1 MT.

Guidance

Almost all SSGW use a form of inertial guidance. It involves three main elements in the GW of which the first is a system to determine which way the missile is pointing in all three planes: this is normally done by three gyros which can measure any movement away from the initial angle of launch. The second element is an accelerometer. If the information from the gyros and the accelerometer is fed into a computer, which in future can be micro-processor based, then it can compute where it is. The third element is another computer which calculates the path the missile should follow, although with current advances in computer technology, it is now possible for one computer to carry out all the calculations.

Before the SSGW is launched, the launching position, the position of the target and the details of the flight path to be followed are fed into the computer. After launch the computers constantly compare the missile's actual position with where it should be if it is following its correct path, and if there is a difference the missile is commanded back on line.

Cruise missiles, and here we are in the misty land of whether a cruise missile is strategic or tactical, use a form of inertial guidance which compares its position with its programmed flight path by matching the terrain contours it is crossing with stored data in the computer. The name given to this system is Terrain Contour Matching (TERCOM). It entails a radar altimeter to determine the contours and it must obviously contain very accurate mapping detail of the ground it is covering. The accuracy of the mapping detail is not released for security reasons by either the United States or USSR, but published material claims an impressive targetting accuracy of 12 m for American cruise missiles. At the moment ranges of up to 2,400 km are claimed for several American cruise missiles and 720 km for the Russian 'Kitchen' Air Launched Cruise Missile (ALCM).

Fig. 11 American Tomahawk ground launched cruise missile (GLCM)

The United States and the USSR both possess ALCMs, Ground Launched Cruise Missiles (GLCMs) and Sea Launched Cruise Missiles (SLCMs). Currently the

United States technology is ahead of the USSR's and there seems little, apart from an advance in air defence systems against low level missiles, or SALT agreements, to stop their development until they take over from long range strike aircraft. The concept has come a long way since its inception in the German V1 flying bomb.

Strategic Missiles

Currently strategic missiles have been developed by China, France, the United States and USSR. The technology is such that it is not the capability to strike with missiles, but the second strike capability which is important in deterrence terms. This means the ability to survive an enemy's strike and strike back. It is this strike back potential which is so important to the deterrence of war. If either side thought that they could strike without the danger of being struck back by a devastating blow, then mutual deterrence would not exist.

The monster ICBMs such as the Russian SS 18 and the American Minuteman III with ranges of over 10,000 miles lie in hardened silos, but as targetting becomes more accurate their survival becomes less certain. The submarine launched American Trident, Russian SS-N-18, French MSBS and British Polaris missiles retain the most assured second strike capability and carry much of the deterrent's credibility. The advent of the SS 20 on its mobile launcher vehicle with a range of up to 4,000 km, shortly to be matched by the American GLCM also on its mobile vehicle, increase the second strike capability. The problem with these weapons is that although Russia is threatened by the American GLCMs in Europe, only Europe is menaced by the SS 20 by virtue of its limited range.

Tactical Weapons

The American Pershing and Sergeant missiles, the French Pluton and the Russian Scaleboard, SS 21 and SS 22 are all examples of tactical missiles. They form a stage in the escalation logic of nuclear weapons. But it is difficult to imagine that a tactical nuclear exchange in densely populated Europe would not be class- ified as strategic by the European countries which suffer, particularly as the war- head yields can reach the megaton level. It may just be possible that some of the shorter range missiles like Lance with its range of 120 miles and its sub-kiloton warhead capability could be used as a short term political warning. It is at this level that perhaps the deterrent logic requires clarification by both sides.

SURFACE TO AIR WEAPON SYSTEMS

There can be little better demonstration of air defence effectiveness than has been seen in the Israeli-Arab wars. Before the Yom Kippur conflict Israeli aircraft ruled the Middle Eastern skies and their ground forces advanced rapidly across the battlefield below. In the Yom Kippur war an Egyptian manned comprehensive air defence system negated the Israeli airforce's effectiveness for a considerable time, until the air defence carpet over Sinai and the Suez canal was torn apart by fierce ground battles. It demonstrated how important an air defence system is.

Elements of an Air Defence System

In a similar way to indirect fire systems described in Chapter 2, an air defence system is made up of many parts, all are important and it takes fine judgement to decide where the most effort should be made. Fig. 12 gives a diagrammatic layout of the system elements.

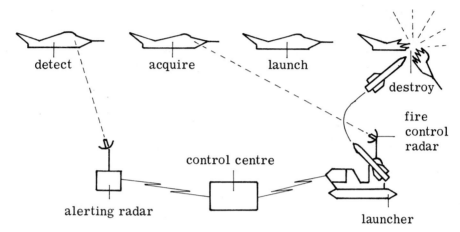

Fig. 12 Elements of an air defence system

As an enemy aircraft approaches it must be detected by an alerting system. It can be as extensive and remarkable as the Ballistic Missile Early Warning System (BMEWS) but is normally more simple for the covering of ground forces when Tactical Control (TC) radars are used. Such radars may be of relatively short range and sited to cover a line or the border of a country; or they may be very large search radars which cover huge areas: the BMEWS radars have a range of over 5,000 km. Whatever their size and siting, their role is to detect incoming enemy aircraft and give as much information about them as possible and alert the control system: they normally also alert the firing units.

Control centres vary from underground bunkers below mountains in the United States or the Urals to an air defence battery control post in a tent. Whatever level they are, they control the states of readiness of the firing units and when sufficient information has been received they allocate targets to firing units. By now it will be apparent that a first class, reliable communication system which can work in EW conditions is an essential ingredient to the system: such communications include satellite links and normal field radios.

When a hostile aircraft is within range, the acquisition devices find and lock on to it. The acquisition is normally performed by fire control (FC) radars, but at lower heights visual trackers, which can be either simple optical or television cameras can be used. IR is employed in several systems for missile tracking. The final part of the air defence system is the missiles: they vary in type, size and in their mountings. They cover from ground level to above 15,000 m (50,000 ft).

Guidance for SAGW

Of all missiles, Surface to Air Guided Weapons (SAGW) use the widest span of guidance systems. They use:

      a   Semi-automatic command to line of sight (SACLOS)
      b   Semi-automatic homing
      c   Passive homing
      d   Automatic command to line of sight (ACLOS)
      e   Beam riding
      f   Command off the line of sight (COLOS).

The first three of these were explained when we considered ATGW.

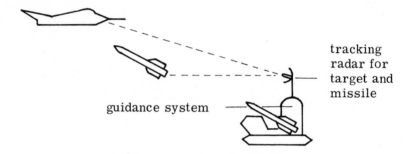

tracking
radar for
target and
missile

guidance system

Fig. 13 Elements of ACLOS system

ACLOS takes the human operator out of the system when the tracker has locked on to the aircraft and the missile has been launched. The tracker notes the line of both the aircraft and the missile: through the guidance computer it commands the missile on to the line of sight to the aircraft. Beam riding is a type of ACLOS in which the missile itself senses when it is off beam and commands itself back on to it. Radar beams were used in the past, but now radar or laser beams may be used.

COLOS guidance is more flexible than any of the other systems because a variety of flight paths for the missiles can be used. The basis of this form of guidance is given in Fig. 14.

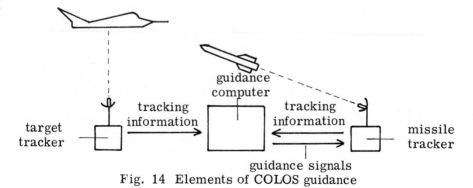

Fig. 14 Elements of COLOS guidance

Separate trackers are used for the missile and the target. They feed continuous information about the positions of both into a guidance computer which sends a continuous stream of commands back to the missile through its tracker until the two flight paths meet as the missile hits the target.

SAGW designed to attack high flying aircraft have far more complex guidance systems, often employing more than one type of guidance, than those which attack low flying aircraft. They are also larger because they need larger propulsion systems.

Weapons for Different Heights

For clarification reasons it is useful to use the NATO height band definitions when looking at the air defence system vertically; they are:

Very low level	-	below 150 m
Low level	-	150 to 600 m
Medium level	-	600 to 7,500 m
High level	-	7,500 to 15,000 m
Very high level	-	above 15,000 m

The very low level weapons provide no more than self defence. At this height band, even small arms can be used. Statistical studies show that there is very little chance of downing a low flying Fighter Ground Attack Aircraft (FGA) nor is there a high chance of causing serious damage to a helicopter unless it is landing

Fig. 15 ZSU 23-4

or taking off well within distance of the small arms. The penalty for firing small arms at aircraft is a high expenditure of ammunition, but it is very good for the morale of the firers and if a pilot sees tracer rising up from the ground he may lose his faith in statistics and not press home his attack. He is even more likely to be deterred if cannons are used against him and the 20 mm cannon on the West German Marder MICV is so designed that it can point upwards at an angle of 1,080 mil (60°). A battalion of Marders firing upwards with tracer rounds could present a formidable deterrent, but again there would be a considerable expenditure of ammunition with little chance of a hit. To give cannons a chance of a hit, they require a good guidance system as indeed the Russian ZSU 23-4 has.

It can engage targets at 2,500 m with an optical guidance sight and at 3,000 m with radar direction. Its rate of fire from its four 23 mm guns is 4,000 rounds per minute which means that it can only fire short bursts if it is not to run out of ammunition very quickly. From Yom Kippur war reports, it appears that the ZSU 23-4 accounted for a considerable percentage of Israeli aircraft when they were forced down within its range by missiles.

The German Gepard mounts two 35 mm guns and it too has radar and optical guidance systems. The main feature of these effective low level air defence guns is their acquisition and guidance systems. At a rough estimate the guns cost one twentieth of the total equipment, the rest is spent on the chassis and especially on the acquisition and guidance systems to ensure that those guns hit the aircraft. Although guns have a very limited range, they have a better ability to engage several targets more quickly than a missile system. The United Kingdom has concentrated entirely on missile systems, partly for economic reasons and partly because missiles have a higher kill probability than guns.

Also in the very low level band are the shoulder launched missiles: the American Redeye and the Russian SA-7 (Grail) are near infra-red homing devices. They are fire and forget missiles but because they home on the heat of the aircraft's engines they are tail chasers and are only effective against FGA which have made their attack. They can home on the heat of a helicopter's engine but engine shielding can foil the homing head.

The British Blowpipe missile is a manual optical MCLOS system much like a first generation ATGW system, but it is commanded by means of a radio link rather than by wire. Its great advantage is its 'forward hitting' capability: it can engage a head-on aircraft, but it must be alerted and acquire the approaching aircraft quickly to be effective. The operator also needs much more training than is required for manning the near-IR homing missiles. The SA 7 can engage an aircraft at a range of 3.6 km up to a height of 1,500 m; the Blowpipe's capability is over 3 km up to a height of 2,000 m.

In the medium level height band there is a wide variety of SAGW, some on tracked carriers and some trailer borne. The main role of all SAGW from the medium band upwards is to provide a carpet of protection, though medium band missiles can also be used for point protection of important targets like bridges or airfields. When deployed for these roles in Europe, where the road systems are extensive, it is difficult to justify the complication and expense of tracked carriers. However for a quick advance, or even when fighting an aggressive delaying battle, forward battle groups may not be under the air defence carpet. In such conditions, tracked carriers could be very useful.

Fig. 16 Blowpipe

Britain is adopting tracked Rapier for this last role, but towed Rapier will remain for the provision of the carpet defence. Rapier reaches out to a range of 7 km and to a height of 3,000 m with both radar and optical guidance. Radar guidance is sometimes very aptly called Blindfire because it gives the missile an effectiveness, not possible with optical guidance, in cloud conditions. As such conditions are very common in Europe, it is a very important capability. The nearest Russian equivalent is the SA-8 (Gecko) which is mounted on a large six wheeled vehicle. It can reach a range of 12 km and a height of 5,000 m.

West Germany and France have adopted the Rolande which is mounted on a tracked carrier. Its range and height capabilities are very similar to Rapier.

Most upper medium, high and very high level SAGW systems are costly and employ either semi-active homing or command off the line of sight systems. The USSR has a very comprehensive family including the SA 6 (Gainful) on its tracked carrier covering up to 13,000 m and the SA 5 (Gammon) with a height ceiling of approximately 30,000 m and a range of 200 km.

Fig. 17 Tracked Rapier

The United States field Chapparal is in the medium height band. In the high/very
high bands Nike Hercules can reach up to 50,000 m and out to 150 km. Hawk is
confined to a height limit of 18,000 m and has a range of approximately 30 km.
The combination of Nike and Hercules provides the upper carpet for the NATO
integrated air defence system (NATINADS). Already, a new missile system,
Patriot, has been developed in the United States to replace the Hawk and Nike
systems. Even more advanced is the Safeguard system which is to protect the
United States from ICBMs. It is composed of two missiles, the long range
Spartan and the shorter range, very fast, Sprint. It is not likely that European
nations will afford to develop such systems.

SUMMARY

GW have developed, since their inception in the German V1, V2 and XH7, faster
than any other form of weapon over the past thirty years. They have influenced
international policies, strategy and tactics to an enormous extent. The technology
involved in the electronic warfare measures and counter measures, which are
mainly beyond the scope and security cover of this chapter, is advancing at an
ever increasing rate. They may yet spell the end of the manned strike aircraft
and our current concept of the MBT.

SELF TEST QUESTIONS

Question 1   What are the advantages and disadvantages of a rocket launcher
              LAW compared with a recoilless LAW?

              Advantages ....

              ....

              Disadvantages ....

              ....

Question 2   What are the advantages to be gained by having a LAW which can-
              not penetrate the frontal armour of a modern MBT?

              Answer ....

              ....

              ....

Question 3   What advantages and disadvantages do ATGW have compared with
              anti-tank guns?

              Advantages ....

              ....

              Disadvantages ....

              ....

              ....

Question 4   What penalties must be paid for increasing the following
              characteristics of an ATGW:

              a   Speed?

                  ....

              b   Range?

                  ....

Question 5   What are the advantages and disadvantages of a semi-active
              homing ATGW compared with a SACLOS missile?

Advantages ....

....

Disadvantages ....

....

Question 6   What are the three main elements of an inertial guidance system?

Answer ....

....

....

Question 7   What gives a cruise missile its degree of invulnerability?

Answer ....

....

Question 8   What are the main elements of a SAGW system?

Answer ....

....

....

....

Question 9   What is the main disadvantage in a very low level SAGW of:
a   A heat seeking warhead?

....

b   A MCLOS guidance system?

....

Question 10   What is the main advantage an AD gun system enjoys compared
with a GW system?

Answer ....

....

ANSWERS ON PAGE   183

Answers to Self Test Questions

CHAPTER 1

Page 30

Question 1   a   Firepower
                   b   Mobility
                   c   Protection.

Question 2   a   Rail movement   eg tunnels and passing
                   b   Road movement   eg bridge classifications.

Question 3   Battlefield mobility is the ability to manoeuvre quickly in and out of action and from bound to bound. Tactical mobility is the ability to move some distance from battle to battle along roads and tracks (some nations refer to this as operational mobility).

Question 4   a   Power to weight ratio
                   b   Ground pressure on tracks
                   c   Design of tracks
                   d   Gear ratios
                   e   Amphibious ability.

Question 5   Advantages   a   Cheaper
                                  b   Lighter
                                  c   Higher muzzle velocity
                                  d   Very suitable for firing fin stabilised ammunition
                                  e   Good for firing HEAT ammunition which should not be spun.

                Disadvantages   f   Fin stabilised rounds are long and more difficult to stow

                                  g   It cannot fire HESH rounds which are too large to be fin stabilised.

Question 6   a   Approximately 20 mm cannon
                   b   Approximately 57 mm rockets
                   c   ATGW eg Hot, Tow, Spiral.

Question 7   a   Anti-tank firepower (not all nations agree)
              b   Anti-light armour capability
              c   More ammunition stowage space for main armament.

Question 8   a   A good surveillance system
              b   Good communications
              c   Good mobility across country
              d   Enough firepower for protection and to fight for information.

Question 9   a   Adequate mobility
              b   Sufficient load carrying capacity
              c   Ease of loading and unloading.

Question 10   a   Motorised raft/bridge like M2
              b   Fascines - palings or tubes
              c   Armoured Vehicle Launched Bridge (AVLB)
              d   Medium Girder Bridge (MGB)
              e   Ribbon Bridge eg Russian PMP.

CHAPTER 2

Page 53

Question 1   a   Weapon and Ammunition
              b   Good surveying (eg use of PADS, LRF)
              c   Good communications
              d   Good control (eg use of computers)
              e   Good target acquisition (eg far IR, Image Intensification, heli-
                  copters, Remotely Piloted Vehicles).

Question 2   Advantages a   Simpler to use
                          b   Lighter
                          c   Higher rate of fire
                          d   More lethal round
                          e   Cheaper
                          f   Less manpower required

              Disadvantages g   Shorter range
                             h   Not so accurate
                             i   More vulnerable to locating radars.

Question 3   a   Not so vulnerable to counter bombardment
              b   More mobile and better cross country performance
              c   Quicker into and out of action
              d   Collective NBC protection
              e   Easier to fit automatic ramming
              f   Swimming capability is possible with smaller SP guns.

Question 4   a   Increase muzzle velocity by having longer barrel
             b   Increase muzzle velocity by increasing propellant power
             c   Use of efficient muzzle brakes
             d   Rocket assisted projectile
             e   Base bleed in projectile
             f   Streamlining of the shell.

Question 5   A high rate of rounds in a short time, say 3 rounds in 8 - 12 secs,
             to land on enemy forces before they are able to take cover. The
             effectiveness of this sudden flurry of rounds is much greater than
             slower rates of fire.

Question 6   a   Rockets
             b   Mortars
             c   Guns.

             Because the lower the launch stresses the better can be the charge
             to mass ratio of the warhead and as a consequence the better will
             be the fragmentation. Rockets can even have pre-notched casings or
             pre-formed fragments, such as ball bearings, set in the warhead
             cases. Finally, the lower the launch stresses the easier it is to
             design carrier warheads containing sub-munitions.

Question 7   Advantages   a   Heavy weight of fire and consequent demoralisation
                          b   Light launcher
                          c   Good warhead lethality
                          d   Good carrier for sub-munitions.

             Disadvantages   e   Strong launch signature
                             f   Large amount of propellant required
                             g   High logistic penalty
                             h   Not so accurate as guns
                             i   Not easy to adjust the range.

Question 8   a   Bomblets and grenadelets
             b   Remotely delivered
             c   Cannon Launched Guided Projectile
             d   Self seeking submunitions eg SADARM.

Question 9   a   Calculation of gun data
             b   Calculation of effects of meteorological conditions
             c   Allocation of targets to guns
             d   Allocation of priorities to targets
             e   Calculation of numbers of rounds for effect
             f   Nature of round to be used bearing in mind availability and
                 location of stocks.

Question 10 a   Longer to increase muzzle velocity
             b   Heavier to absorb recoil, absorb heat, counter bending and
                 withstand high pressure
             c   Will have fume extractor
             d   May have thermal jacket.

CHAPTER 3

Page 73

Question 1 a Quick Firing (QF)
            b Recoilless (RCL)
            c Breech Loading (BL) or Separate Case.

Question 2 a Cap
            b Primer
            c Main propellant.

Question 3 a To fire APFSDS rounds. These were developed to achieve a
               long narrow rod, which would be unstable if spun

            b To fire HEAT rounds: the effect of the HEAT jet is degraded if
               spun

            c To achieve high muzzle velocities.

Question 4 The HESH warhead is large and heavy. The addition of a tail and
            fins to fin stabilise it would lead to a very long round.

Question 5 A HEAT warhead's armour penetration is approximately three or
            four times the diameter of the cone, but this may well be improved
            upon in the future.

Question 6 a Anti-armour sub-munitions
            b Belly attack mines, whether laid by hand or scattered.

Question 7 a Smokes
            b Illuminating
            c Incendiary
            d Flare cannister
            e Propaganda
            f Nuclear
            g Radar echo
            h Sub-munition such as bomblets, grenadelets, minelets and self-
               seeking anti-armour devices.

Question 8 a Reliability
            b Safety

Question 9 a Cutting tracks or blowing off the wheels by blast
            b Attacking the belly by blast or Miznay Schardin device
            c Attacking the side by off-route mines using hollow charge or
               Miznay Schardin warheads.

Question 10 a Laying by hand
            b Laying by mechanical means eg Barmine Layer
            c Scattering from launcher eg Ranger
            d Scattering from helicopter

    e   Scattering from carrier shells - RDMs.

CHAPTER 4

Page 91

Question 1	a	Blast
	b	Thermal
	c	Radiation.

Question 2	a	Crushing by the overpressure
	b	Overturning or blowing down by wind
	c	Eardrum bursting by overpressure of over 15 psi
	d	Injury by being blown against some hard object
	e	Injury by being hit by flying debris.

Question 3	a	Blinding either temporarily or permanently. This could cause loss of control of a vehicle or aircraft.
	b	Burns from the flash
	c	Flame effects which cause materials to catch fire.

Question 4	a	Alpha particles - 2 neutrons + 2 protons
	b	Beta particles - electron
	c	Gamma radiation - short electromagnetic waves
	d	Neutron radiation - stream of neutrons.

Question 5	a	200 - 500 rads: incapacitation after one week, many deaths
	b	500 - 1,000 rads: incapacitation after 4 days, most would die.

Question 6	a	Denial of ground
	b	Denial of transit if severe enough.

Question 7	a	Radiation
	b	Thermal

Question 8	a	Radiation
	b	Blast

Question 9	a	To deny ground
	b	To deny transit through an area

To create immediate neutralisation prior to an attack on concentrations of troops

Question 10	a	Oximes as a prophylactic
	b	Atropine as a therapy.

CHAPTER 5

Page 113

Question 1   a   It is shorter
              b   It is lighter
              c   It has a shorter range
              d   It is less lethal.

Question 2   The smaller mass is compensated by a higher muzzle velocity.

Question 3   a   One weapon which can fulfil the function of both the rifle and the
                  LMG eg Galil

              b   A light weight rifle and a relatively heavy LMG or GPMG
              c   Two similar weapons, but one with a better sustained rate of fire
                  eg RPK and AKM.

Question 4   a   The weapon becomes too hot to handle
              b   Cook off occurs if the round is kept in the chamber
              c   The barrel quickly wears out.

Question 5   Advantages   a   Can put down a good volume of fire to help win the
                               fire fight

                           b   Can produce high volume of fire in the defence.

              Disadvantages c   Less accurate than single shot weapon
                             d   Uses more ammunition
                             e   More complicated drills required.

Question 6   Consistency is the ability to produce a tight grouping of shots.
              Accuracy is the application of shots so they land at or very near the
              point at which the sights are aimed.

Question 7   Advantages   a   Magnification leading to accuracy
                           b   Better at low light levels
                           c   The eye only has to focus on one plane as opposed to
                               three (backsight, foresight and target).

              Disadvantages d   Size
                             e   Weight
                             f   Bulk
                             g   Cost
                             h   A small field of view which results in a relatively
                                 long time to locate the target in the sight.

Question 8   a   It must not protrude so far from the armour that it is vulnerable
              b   The barrel should be easy to change and it should be possible to
                  withdraw the barrel rearwards

              c   Fumes should be discharged outside the vehicle.

Question 9   An Air Defence cannon should have a high rate of fire, while an anti-light armour cannon should, ideally, be a single shot weapon.

Question 10   a   Self protection
               b   Close quarter fighting.

CHAPTER 6

Page 135

Question 1   Because it would take up a bandwidth of approximately 5.5 MHz. This bandwidth could accommodate 250 VHF FM voice channels.

Question 2   Advantages   a   Greater range. Much greater if sky-wave is used.
                                 b   Not so easily subject to screening by foliage, buildings or hills.
                                 c   Less bandwidth required because it uses AM.

            Disadvantages   d   Subject to noise
                                 e   Subject to interference
                                 f   Its range makes it less secure
                                 g   Larger antenna required
                                 h   Less easy to use for re-broadcasting
                                 i   Worse speech quality
                                 j   No 'capture effect'.

Question 3   a   Common audio gear, batteries and battery charging
               b   Common operating techniques
               c   Common maintenance features
               d   Interoperability
               e   No interference when fitted in the same vehicle
               f   Common ruggedness to allow them all to be used in the same extreme conditions.

Question 4   a   They are cheaper
               b   They can be used in the less demanding environments such as Internal Security and protection duties

               c   They may use more modern technology
               d   With a central booster they can be small and use small power supplies.

Question 5   a   Secure voice
               b   Teleprinter
               c   Computer data
               d   Facsimile.

Question 6   Because it has a matrix of nodes which allow messages to travel by a variety of routes, some of which can be destroyed without breaking all communication paths.

Question 7   a   The Commander and staff are kept up to date with information
             b   A very quick transfer of command is possible
             c   Print outs can eliminate many state boards
             d   The information is the same in each store
             e   Computer data can replace voice traffic
             f   Many returns become unnecessary.

Question 8   a   ESM - The gaining of information about an enemy and his equip-
                 ment by electronic means

             b   ECM - Preventing an enemy from using his electronic equipment
                 effectively

             c   ECCM - Preventing the enemy using ECM against us.

Question 9   a   Detection, and listening, equipments
             b   Jamming equipments

Question 10 a   Use minimum transmitting range. Only use high power boost
                 when essential

             b   Change frequency as often as feasible
             c   Use radio silence
             d   Cut transmissions down to a minimum
             e   Use 'burst transmissions'
             f   Site radios and especially RR terminals carefully
             g   Use narrow transmission beams if possible.

CHAPTER 7

Page 151

Question 1   a   Detection
             b   Recognition
             c   Identification
             d   Location.

Question 2   Advantages   a   Long range
                           b   Penetrates smoke, rain and mist very well
                           c   Measures distance
                           d   Measures speed.

             Disadvantages e   It is active and so is detectable
                            f   It cannot, as yet, provide a clear picture
                            g   It cannot, as yet, be used as a sight.

Question 3   Speed of pulse is 300,000,000 m/sec

             Time of pulse to target and return is $\dfrac{1}{15,000}$ sec

             Therefore distance travelled is $\dfrac{300,000,000}{15,000}$ m = 20,000 m

Therefore distance to target is half that ie $\dfrac{20,000}{2}$ = 10,000 m

Therefore distance to target = 10 Km.

Question 4   a   They are good at looking through rain, mist and smoke, but not so good as radar

              b   They have reasonable ranges which match those of tank guns and ATGW

              c   They provide a recognisable picture and can be used as a sight
              d   They are passive and so not easy to detect.

Question 5   It is a telescope with an image intensification tube fitted into it. The tube intensifies or amplifies the light by 40,000 times or more.

Question 6   Advantages   a   Light weight for short ranges
                              b   Can pick out low level lights, such as side-lights, at great distances

                              c   Can see near IR lights as white light
                              d   It is passive
                              e   It can be used as a sight for short range weapons.

              Disadvantages   f   It can not see through rain, mist and smoke
                              g   It does not measure range or speed.

Question 7   a   Range finding
             b   Designating targets for guided weapons.

Question 8   Communications. This will probably be mainly used in conjunction with fibre optic cables.

Question 9   It can see over the horizon, probably out to a range of sixty or seventy kilometres.

Question 10   a   Seismic
              b   Thermal
              c   Magnetic
              d   Acoustic.

CHAPTER 8

Page 173

Question 1   Advantages   a   It is lighter
                              b   It can have a disposable launcher. (This causes problems for accurate sighting).

              Disadvantages   c   It is longer
                              d   It has a shorter range.

Question 2   a It can be lighter
              b It can have a greater range
              c It can certainly be operated by one man. (It is not impossible,
                 however, that a LAW which can penetrate the frontal armour of
                 a MBT could also be carried by one man, but it is difficult to
                 achieve).

Question 3   Advantages   a Light weight
                           b Range

              Disadvantages c Rate of fire
                             d Normally only one type of warhead (though HESH
                                warheads have also been known on ATGW)

                             e Slower speed of engagement (due to relative slow
                                time of flight of ATGW).

Question 4   a Weight, because a larger boost motor is required
              b Weight, because a larger sustain motor is required.

Question 5   Advantages   a Separation of launcher from control
                           b Speeds up re-engagement by launcher

              Disadvantages c Cost
                             d Need for communications system between launcher
                                and guidance.

Question 6   a System to determine which way the missile is pointing
              b A system to determine its acceleration
              c Computer(s) to calculate the desired path and compare the actual
                 position of the missile. This decides the path correction required.

Question 7   a Its low flight altitude
              b Its ability to vary from a straight line path.

Question 8   a A detection and alerting system
              b A target acquisition system
              c A control centre
              d A missile

Question 9   a It can only engage after the aircraft has passed and completed its
                 attack

              b It requires considerable operator training.

Question 10   It can engage several targets more quickly than a GW system (Multi-
              target engagement capability).

Glossary of Abbreviations

A

ACLOS	-	Automatic Command to Line of Sight
AFV	-	Air Launched Cruise Missile
AM	-	Amplitude Modulated
AP	-	Armour Piercing
APC	-	Armoured Personnel Carrier
APDS	-	Armour Piercing Discarding Sabot
APFSDS	-	Armour Piercing Fin Stabilised Discarding Sabot
ATGW	-	Anti-Tank Guided Weapon
AVLB	-	Armoured Vehicle Launched Bridge
AVRE	-	Armoured Vehicle Royal Engineers

B

Bde	-	Brigade
BE	-	Base Ejection
BL	-	Breech Loading
BMEWS	-	Ballistic Missile Early Warning System

C

CFS	-	Close Fire Support
COLOS	-	Command Off Line of Sight
CLOS	-	Command to Line of Sight
CRT	-	Cathode Ray Tube
CT	-	Combat Team
CW	-	Chemical Warfare

D

Div   -   Division
DFS   -   Depth Fire Support

E

ECM   -   Electronic Counter Measures
ECCM   -   Electronic Counter Counter Measures
EHF   -   Extra High Frequency
EMP   -   Electro-Magnetic Pulse
ESM   -   Electronic Support Measures
EW   -   Electronic Warfare
EWCC   -   Electronic Warfare Control Centre
EWLO   -   Electronic Warfare Liaison Officer

F

FACE   -   Field Artillery Computing Equipment
FC Radar   -   Fire Control Radar
FEBA   -   Forward Edge of the Battle Area
FFR   -   Free Flight Rocket
FGA   -   Fighter Ground Attack Aircraft
FM   -   Frequency Modulated
FOO   -   Forward Observation Officer
FPF   -   Final Protective Fire

G

g   -   gram
GHz   -   Gigahertz
GLCM   -   Ground Launched Guided Missile
GPMG   -   General Purpose Machine Gun
GZ   -   Ground Zero

H

HE   -   High Explosive
HEAT   -   High Explosive Anti-Tank

HEP	-	High Explosive Plastic
HESH	-	High Explosive Squash Head
HF	-	High Frequency
HMLC	-	High Mobility Load Carrier
Hz	-	Hertz

I

ICM	-	Improved Conventional Munition
IFCS	-	Improved Fire Control Sustem
IR	-	Infra Red
IW	-	Individual Weapon
IWS	-	Individual Weapon Sight

K

kg	-	kilogram
KE	-	Kinetic Energy
KHz	-	Kilohertz
KT	-	Kiloton

L

LAW	-	Light Anti-Tank Weapon
LF	-	Low Frequency
LMG	-	Light Machine Gun
LMLC	-	Low Mobility Load Carrier
LRATGW	-	Long Range Anti-Tank Guided Weapon
LRF	-	Laser Range Finder
LSW	-	Light Support Weapon

M

MBT	-	Main Battle Tank
MCLOS	-	Manual Command to Line of Sight
MF	-	Medium Frequency
MGB	-	Medium Girder Bridge
MHE	-	Mechanical Handling Equipment
MHz	-	Megahertz

MICV	-	Mechanised Infantry Combat Vehicle
MLRS	-	Multi Launch Rocket System
MMG	-	Medium Machine Gun
MMLC	-	Medium Mobility Load Carrier
MPI	-	Mean Point of Impact
MT	-	Megaton

N

NAIAD	-	Nerve Agent Immobilised Enzyme Alarm and Detection

O

OP	-	Observation Post

P

PADS	-	Position and Azimuth Determining System
psi	-	Pounds per Square Inch

Q

QF	-	Quick Firing

R

RAP	-	Rocket Assisted Projectile
RDM	-	Remotely Delivered Mine
RECS	-	Radio Electronic Combat Support
RCL	-	Recoilless
RP	-	Red Phosphorous
RPV	-	Remotely Piloted Vehicle
RR	-	Radio Relay
RVD	-	Residual Vapour Detector
RX	-	Receiver

S

SACLOS	-	Semi Active Command to Line of Sight
SADARM	-	Seek and Destroy ARMour
SAGW	-	Surface to Air Guided Weapon
SALT	-	Strategic Arms Limitation Talks
SCRA	-	Single Channel Radio Access
SHF	-	Super High Frequency
SLCM	-	Sea Launched Cruise Missile
SMG	-	Sub Machine Gun
SOPs	-	Standing Operating Procedures
SP gun	-	Self Propelled gun
SSGW	-	Surface to Surface Guided Weapon

T

TC radar	-	Tactical Control Radar
TREE	-	Transient Radiation Effect on Electronics
TX	-	Transmitter

U

UGS	-	Unattended Ground Sensors
UHF	-	Ultra High Frequency

V

VDU	-	Visual Display Unit
VHF	-	Very High Frequency
VMMG	-	Vehicle Mounted Machine Gun
VT fuze	-	Variable Time fuze

W

WP	-	White Phosphorus

Index

191